Recipe for Disaster

HOW A SIMPLE IDEA GREW INTO A MILLION-DOLLAR BUSINESS, TRANSFORMING THE INVENTOR ALONG THE WAY

Melissa Coleman

Copyright © 2014 by Melissa Coleman
All rights reserved.
ISBN: 0989422801
ISBN 13: 978-0989422802

The names of some people portrayed in this book have been changed to protect their privacy.

Dedicated to My Father:
The inventor of forty-eleven things

Sara?
Yeah, Mom?
What's the most important thing you will ever have to learn how to manage?
Relationships, Mom. You've told me this like a zillion times.
That's right, honey. Relationships.

A NECESSARY DISCLAIMER —

I might have been the one to scream the loudest, but I was not the only one to scream.

I might have been the first to change, but I was not the only one who changed.

He did too.

It is not easy to radically accept that none of us can ultimately control our lives or the people in them. All we can control are our reactions and our plan for going forward.

You deserve more credit than you get. You have shown extraordinary patience, and, wonderfully, became the father you surprised yourself you could be.

For everything—thank you.

CONTENTS

A Necessary Disclaimer — · VII
Introduction · XI
Part I · 1
    1   Math · 1
    2   Looks Like Stormy Weather · · · · · · · · · · · · · · · · · · · 11
    3   Every Other Thursday · 19
    4   Channel Surfing · 29
    5   Basket Case · 39
Part II · 47
    6   Insomnia Is a Form Of Torture · · · · · · · · · · · · · · · · · · 47
    7   Final Score: Cancer 2, Mom 1 · · · · · · · · · · · · · · · · · · 57
    8   Keep. Throw Away. Goodwill. · · · · · · · · · · · · · · · · · · 77
    9   Tidy Boxes · 83
Part III · 93
    10   Honey, Target Called Today · · · · · · · · · · · · · · · · · · · 93
    11   Peter V. Paul · 99
    12   What Happens Over Vegas · 105
    13   Pacing The Floor · 113
    14   Leap Of Unfaith · 123
    15   Our Dog Is Dead, and So Is Our Marriage · · · · · · · · 133
    16   Shock At 200 Joules · 141
Part IV · 149
    17   Feeling My Way in the Dark · · · · · · · · · · · · · · · · · · 149
    18   Kismet · 155
    19   Bankruptcy Can Kiss My Ass · · · · · · · · · · · · · · · · · · 167

Conclusion · 169
Acknowledgments · 171
About The Author · 173

INTRODUCTION

Meatloaf…

Let's think about meatloaf for a moment. Lots of positives: it's solid. Good. Simple. The easiest thing in the world to prepare. Some ground meat, an egg, a handful of breadcrumbs, ketchup, season to taste. Tasty. Predictable. Fundamental to a "meat and potatoes" life. Relatively nutritious.

Basically, only a single downside: boring as hell.

How many nights a week can you eat meatloaf? Really? Unless circumstances don't allow you to put anything else on the table, what does meatloaf say about you? About who you are? About your life?

The upside? You're solid. Good. Simple. Predictable.

The downside?

The sad thing is, most of us live the equivalent of "meatloaf" lives. Plodding along in our simple, solid, predictable ways.

A meatloaf life's ingredients are straightforward. The right amount of school. A dash of talent. Some smarts, but not too much. Good-enough-looking but not stunning. A little luck. Season to taste with conventional dreams and goals.

Isn't that the recipe most of us use when we put our lives together, our simple, meatloaf lives? We take these decent, modest ingredients, and we put together a simple, modest, and conventional life.

We try to be good kids. We do our homework and have goals that will make our parents proud. We go to college. We fall in love. We get married. We have kids. We get a house. We put up the white picket fence and mow the lawn. We hope the neighbors don't think we're weird. We want people to think our marriages are perfect or, if not perfect, just dandy. *We* want to think our marriages are perfect. We want our kids to be proud of us...We love being proud of our kids.

Approximately seven years in, we begin to see our husbands and wives in a new light. And maybe they don't look quite as wonderful in that light. Rather than look too closely, though, we distract ourselves. We tinker in the garage. We remodel the kitchen. We host backyard barbecues. We get a few more dogs, cats, and hamsters for the kids. We get caught up in their lives ad nauseam. We max ourselves with commitments. We drink a bit more than we should. We do everything we can to ignore the itch that is nagging us—everything we can to not come face-to-face with the truth, which is that we cannot find comfort in the simple—sometimes successful—lives that we've worked so hard to create for ourselves.

Maybe that isn't what happens to everyone, or even most people. But I think it happens to way more people than you would imagine. And it sure as hell happened to me: big time. I didn't just get tired of the meatloaf life, I got exhausted with it. I couldn't take another step with its weight on my shoulders and my soul. It wasn't because I *wanted* to get tired of it. Not because I wished to become uncomfortable in it. Not because I ever lost sight of the fundamental decency and goodness of my meatloaf life. The truth is, it devastated me that I couldn't stomach my recipe any more. It broke my heart in ways that still hurt me to this day. I didn't want to not be satisfied with what I had. I never wanted it to happen, never asked for it to happen.

But happen, it did.

My carefully constructed, simple life seemed to come crashing down on me all at once—"seemed to" because I'd done such a good job at ignoring the clues and convincing myself that all was well.

But one day I literally awoke to the realization that I was living my parents' life—a bland but healthy dish graciously handed down with love and good intentions. I had gathered all the ingredients and dutifully made the main course. However...It wasn't my recipe. It wasn't my meal.

I had reached a point where I knew that if I tried to make myself eat one more bite of that kind of life, I was going to choke to death right then and there on my kitchen floor.

I couldn't do it anymore. I just couldn't. I couldn't, I couldn't.

I'm not necessarily proud of *how* I thrashed my way out of my conventional life. The sum-total collateral damage was more than I ever would have known at the time. But. I am proud of how I came out on the other side. I am proud of my family. I kicked and clawed my way, going against just about everything I'd ever thought my life would be or had been taught about how I should behave. I am convinced that I made every selfish mistake along the way. I think back on the path that has led me to here, and there are way too many moments that mortify me, shame me, and embarrass me. But the one emotion that never surfaces…is regret.

Somehow, someway, I was able to come out on the other end of my jagged struggle for myself smelling like a rose, not only creating, but then selling a successful business and laying the foundation for a wonderful, healthy family. An angel somewhere shone a light on me. A gem of an idea was given to me, somehow gifted into my consciousness. A one-in-a-million success story became my own. Not by a road map or a conscious strategy, but through perseverance, borderline-annoying tenacity, a deep knowledge that there was no going back, and, most of all, an extreme, undying passion.

It's not easy or pretty to fight your way out of the warm, safe, infuriating, and confining cocoon that has been all you have known your entire life. I'm pretty damned sure there is no good way to do it. If there is, I sure as hell hadn't figured it out when I was going through it. But that process, that ability to be creative, to *do* something, to be that person you have ceased to know (or possibly never met), and to respect or to like her…That's good.

That's damned good.

I created something from that chaos of confusion and unhappiness. I think a lot of people who create things, whether it's a painting, a novel, a poem, a start-up business, a nonprofit, or a new device, technology, or software are pushed forward by the same things, the same urges, the same determination not to give in when you finally realize that life just can't be only what it seems.

There has to be more! I have to give more!

There is.

I can.

My mother once said to me as we were driving down the road—me the driver, her the passenger—a year out of cancer remission and two years before she died, "You girls (meaning women, but always 'girls' to her)…you try to do too much today. You take on too many things. It was simpler in my time."

She was right. Life often does seem more complicated today. So many choices. So much noise. So many distractions. I was trying to do, be, become, and achieve too much, striving for a goal I couldn't even see, let alone explain. But it pulled me. What might have seemed to be "too much" was a gravitational pull, pulling me to my true self.

She then paused and looked out the window with an intent stare that looked far beyond the trees whizzing by in a blur on the country road and said, "But honey. You really should write a book someday."

Oh Mom—now *there's* a recipe that makes sense to me.

Christopher Columbus to David Ponder:

"Getting started, getting finished—both ends of a journey require a demonstration of passion," Columbus mused. *David stared blankly at the great man. "Passion!" he said again in a forceful whisper. "Passion is a product of the heart. Passion is what helps you when you have a great dream. Passion breeds conviction and turns mediocrity into excellence! Your passion will motivate others to join you in pursuit of your dream. With passion, you will overcome insurmountable obstacles. You will become unstoppable!"*

—*The Traveler's Gift,* Andy Andrews

Part I

Chapter 1

MATH

The cycle of life.

Girls are born to grow up and become mommies. Birth to give birth, nurture, and love. June 1, 2001: I was in a naïve, synchronistic harmony with that cycle of life. I felt that everything about my life was perfect. I was going "home" to deliver the happiest news I could imagine.

I was going back to the town and home I had grown up in, to tell my mom that she was going to be a grandmother.

Whatever unhappiness my mom felt in her life, this would resonate deeply and happily with her. This would make everything perfect. Whatever hurt she felt in her life, I knew this would ease it; whatever disappointment or void, this would fill it.

Like a four-year-old on Christmas morning, I practically hopped out of bed the day we were going. Everything that day is etched in my memory. I remember sitting up on the edge of my bed and planting my feet on the tan shag-carpeted floor and pausing before getting up. "This is the day," I thought to myself. "I can't wait to tell my mom!"

I knew that there was no better present in the world that I could give her. It was all I could do not to call ahead to give her the news. But that would ruin the wonderful fantasy I'd conjured up in my mind. I could practically see the look on my mom's face when I told her. "Oh

Lissa, that's wonderful!" I heard her say in my mind's ear. It brought tears of joy to my eyes.

"Morning," Benny said, coming into the room to check on me and finding me sitting on the bed, staring vacantly into space.

I smiled a million-dollar smile at him. He was my guy, the father of the baby already growing in my belly.

"Want some coffee?"

I shook my head and made a "gag-me" face.

He nodded, seeming to understand my feelings perfectly. "I'll get you a bowl of Cheerios," he said, knowing it was one of the few things I could eat when I was feeling queasy from morning sickness. "OJ?"

"Small glass," I said.

He turned toward the kitchen to meet me there.

"Love you," I called after him. Then I took a few deep, relaxing breaths. Outside, the sun was already shining. It was a beautiful spring day. The birds were chirping outside my window. Mary Poppins may well have been dancing with me around the house singing and frolicking. Bliss!

What a sweet, sweet moment I anticipated: telling my mom that she would be a grandmother. I knew how she'd been longing, wishing, craving to be a grandmother. Her girlfriends all had grandchildren, and they were always showing her pictures at the local diner, bragging about how cute they were.

Mom would smile a tight, polite smile as she endured the bragging, always asking sweetly how everyone was doing. Inside, she was growing more and more desperate to have a grandchild of her own.

"Are you and Benny thinking of starting a family?" she would ask me.

"What's the rush?" I'd tease her.

"Oh. I'm not trying to rush you, and it's not my business, honey. I'm just asking."

Yeah, right. Neither my older sister nor I had given her a grandchild yet, and she was dying to have one to fuss over. I'm sure visions of buying sweet pink dresses with ruffles floated in her imagination. And now, as I settled into the passenger seat of the car, her baby was coming home to tell her she was having a baby! Her dream would be coming true.

I knew her life with my dad wasn't always easy. Like most women of her generation, she'd put up with a lot. Her focus had been on raising her children and keeping a good home. In my heart of hearts, I knew she was unhappy sometimes, felt controlled by my father, but I chose to focus on the smile she showed me, not anything else.

Benny and I laughed and sang with the radio on the drive up. The dog panted and fidgeted in the backseat, leaving drool marks on the center console. Halfway, we stopped at a deli in Rutland, Vermont, to get something to eat. I was feeling much better and felt famished.

We sat outside and enjoyed our bagel sandwiches until we became antsy to get back on the road. In between our laughing and choosing music, we talked like I imagine most young couples with a baby on the way talk, about "things that matter." Making lists. Making plans. Unearthing dreams.

"What're the most important things to you in life?" Benny asked me. He glanced over. "In order of priority."

I smiled. "You mean, after you?"

"Ha ha," he said. "Of course I mean after me."

I thought for a moment. Then I shrugged. "That the baby's all right, I guess."

Benny was quiet. Thoughtful. Just like him, I thought to myself. Considering these "important things" carefully. I smiled to myself.

We ended up with a list of about five important things in life. "I think health is the most important thing," he said finally. "Because without that, everything else is more difficult."

I put my hand on his leg. I couldn't have agreed more. He was so logical and sensible. So good. We agreed that health was the most important thing. Yep, that was it. Health.

How young we were! How innocent! Talking about "things that mattered," oblivious to how the passage of time would warp and change everything, oblivious to how quickly anything could darken the joy we felt, to the fact that things were just about to become unraveled, just around the corner of our lives.

It seemed like we had only just gotten into the car and there we were, pulling up the long dirt driveway to the house. The very driveway I'd run up and down a million times, the one where I had played with my Matchbox cars in the mud for hours as a little girl, did cartwheels, and learned to ride a bike. The one where a thousand memories resided, still living among the pebbles and stones and floating under the tall pine trees lining the gravel.

I spotted Dad down in the back yard near the shed, a field of green grass between us. I started waving through the glass. He looked up at the sound of the car. A genuine smile creased his face. He gave a small wave and then started across the lawn to meet us.

"Hey, Tiger," he said, hugging me as I got out of the car. He reached out to shake Benny's hand when he came around the car to join us. A real man-to-man greeting.

Not an inkling of anything amiss. My life equaled a scene from a Foldgers Coffee Christmas commercial. There we were, saying hi, Dad asking about the drive, Benny reaching to get our stuff from the car… perfect.

Our golden retriever, Tommy, hopped out of the car as Benny opened the door and ran around the yard, sniffing each and every tree, searching for the perfect place to pee. Dad smiled and then, with an arm around my shoulders, led us toward the back porch.

The screened-in porch was exactly as it had always been—welcoming, comfortable, and relaxing. We had a view of the hilltops that was the envy of the neighbors.

"Where's Mom?" I asked, looking forward to seeing her and telling her my news.

"Oh, she'll be down in a minute," Dad said, waving vaguely in the direction of the house. "Can I get you anything?" He looked over at Benny. "Something to drink? A beer?"

We both shook our heads as we settled into the cushioned chairs on the screened-in porch, gently smirking at one another, knowing the news we were about to share.

"Good to be out of the car," Benny said, stretching his legs out.

I reached my arms up and stretched. "It is," I agreed. The smile on my face was almost too much to contain.

Just then, there was a noise at the sliding door between the dining room and the porch. I looked over. "Oh, there you are!" I said, smiling and starting to get up. "Hi, Mom!"

She stopped before coming through the door. The daylight streaming into the porch was bright, so she was a bit lost in the relative darkness of the indoors behind her. My eyes tried to adjust to the mixture of light and shadow where she stood.

"We couldn't wait to get here," I said, crossing the porch and heading for the door.

She smiled and gave me a gentle hug even as I wrapped my arms around her and gave her a tight embrace. I noticed that her greeting was not what it normally would be. Her usual fashion was to come right out onto the porch and give both of us a big hug and greet us in her soft, soothing voice. My mother—there was not a mean bone in her petite body, always pleasant and polite.

It took a second to register, but she seemed reluctant to come outside.

"Come out on the porch, Mom." She didn't move. A shiver passed through me: some unspoken message. A red flag. Danger. Warning. "What's the matter? Is something wrong?"

Standing just outside on the porch, the bright sun all around me and the darker room behind her, I couldn't see her well. But now I knew something was wrong. Something was troubling her. I studied her face. She wouldn't look up from the floor. She was clearly troubled about something.

She shook her head. "Nothing," she said unconvincingly. "Nothing's wrong." Then she turned from the doorway and headed back inside. "Nothing," she said again, her voice quivering. Then, over her shoulder she added, "But come into the living room. Please."

I felt my heart sink. Something was wrong. Would the news of my baby be able to fix whatever was upsetting her? "God damn it," I thought to myself. "They must be getting divorced! Why now?" I thought, maybe she's just feeling older. Maybe his controlling had finally become too much. Maybe it really frustrated her about not having a grandchild. Maybe she'd just gotten fed up without any kind of buffer in the house.

I knew she wasn't happy. She bristled more and more about how she didn't feel she could do anything on her own. The last time she'd visited, her frustration was more in the open than I'd ever seen it before. I mean, Jesus, this was a woman whose husband had pumped the gas in her car every Thursday for the last thirty years. How much more could one woman take of having no voice, no independence?

"Oh shit," I thought to myself as I followed her into the living room. I drew a couple of deep breaths and then reached back to grab Benny's hand. I squeezed it as we walked into the living room together. I prepared myself for the worst. They were going to separate.

OK, that was sad. But it wasn't *that* bad, I assured myself. A little independence could be a good thing. She could live with us for a while. It would be great for her to be there to help when the baby came.

When we got to the living room, Mom sat in her usual spot on the big brown couch. Dutifully, Dad sat in his spot on the little couch. Ben sat with Dad on the other end of the little couch. Everyone was in his or her place. For some reason, I broke pattern. I sat in the 1969 rocking chair with gold cushions in the far corner of the living room. No one had sat in the rocking chair for ages, but there are photographs of Mom sitting in the chair as she cradled and rocked both my sister and me as babies.

I kept my eyes down, wondering if my teeny-tiny belly bump might be noticeable, which, of course it couldn't be yet. When I raised them, I looked over at Mom. I could feel my eyes widen. In the light of the room, I could see her more clearly now. It was obvious that something was wrong. Her skin. Her face. It looked different.

Her skin was…It was…yellow.

"Mom?"

She looked away.

I turned to my dad. "What's wrong?"

He looked down at the floor. I looked questioningly at Benny. He looked confused and shrugged, so I turned back to my mom. "Mom, what is it?" I could hear the panic in my voice. Something weighing a thousand pounds fell from my throat to my stomach, a wave of uncomfortable heat replacing it.

I braced myself for the words, "Melissa, honey, your dad and I are getting divorced…" I almost believed I could hear those words and deal with them OK. I would say, "Well, I can top that. I'm pregnant, Mom!" Our news will surely hold everyone and everything together.

I was ready to hear that message. But no one said anything. The quiet was frightening. It was probably only a few seconds, but it felt interminable. Then Mom cleared her throat. I looked right at her. She looked away and then shifted her eyes so that she was looking down at the floor again.

"I haven't been feeling very good lately."

Being a nurse, I know that starting a conversation with something like that is *never* a good thing. I could feel my body go numb.

"I…uh…um…" She took a big breath.

I could see how hard it was for her to say what she had to say, but even now I can only begin to imagine just how unbearably hard it must have really been. When she did finally manage to begin to speak, it was without emotion, by rote, like she'd been rehearsing what she was going to say over and over and over again.

"I've been having this pain in my abdomen. I thought it was just a stomach bug, but then I went to Dr. Clancy." She started to twirl the edge of her shirt in her fingers in a repetitive motion.

"She sent me for some tests. They did an ultrasound and found a tumor…" Here her voice caught, and I thought she was going to stop talking so my father could take it from there. But she gathered herself, put her shoulders back, and blurted the rest out. "It's on my pancreas. I have cancer. Dr. Clancy says I have three to six months to live. She sent me home with some Xanax and told me to start making my arrangements."

Three to six months…three to six months…three to six months was all I heard echoing in my head.

Oh my God, oh my God, oh my God! You've got to be fucking kidding me! Take it back. Take it back! Tell me you're leaving dad. Tell me you have to sell the house. Tell me *anything* but that! No, no, no, no!

My peripheral vision went foggy, quickly forming what I can only describe as a white triangular tunnel in front of me. Time stopped, and the entire world outside the triangle of the big couch, the small couch, and the rocking chair disappeared.

Her voice, the soft voice that had comforted me, supported me, advised me, said she loved me—that voice was echoing in my mind, distorted and grotesque.

I couldn't move.

There was no time. No sensation. Nothing. Just a white hollow space in front of me.

"…the yellow is from being jaundiced. It's the tumor blocking the ducts…four and a half centimeters"…echoing…echoing…

I knew all about tumors and ducts and blockages. I know what pancreatic cancer is! It's a fucking death sentence.

"Dad and I have had a tough few weeks…"

Then Dad's voice was somewhere in the room. Talking about something. Doctor visits. Tests. Driving Mom places. Treatments. Decisions that had to be made. Calling a surgeon.

Three to six months. Cancer. Pancreas. Tumor. Three to six months.

I looked at Ben. My strong, brave man. Benny, who had confronted all sorts of horrible things in his job and could still come home and kiss me, had a look of horror in his eyes. Benny, save me! But I could see in his eyes that he felt as lost as me. He looked stunned. His lip quivered. Benny, who probably hadn't cried since he was six years old. I could see my own pain reflected in his eyes. And it was then that my tears started. And not just crying, but waves of salty tears streaming down my face and out my nose. Uncontrollably. My body was wracked, but the rocking chair didn't move. My hands were death-gripped to the arms of that 1969 rocking chair.

The joy of anticipation I'd felt that morning was gone. Destroyed. Obliterated. Impossible and cruel. The sound of a pounding heart echoed in my head.

I was sobbing, and in my head I was trying to accomplish one very simple arithmetic equation. I was six weeks pregnant, almost two months. OK, nine months minus two months. Nine minus two equals seven. Seven months until you'll be a grandmother!

"I have three to six months…"

The math didn't work. It didn't fucking work! She wasn't going to live long enough to see her first grandchild. What horrible, cosmic, fucked-up kind of joke was this? You've got to be kidding me!

This is not the way it is supposed to be.

Oh my God, what should I do? Tell her what I'd come home to tell her, that she's going to be a grandmother? I can't do that to her. I can't. It would crush her. It will devastate her even more. If that's even possible.

I would like to say that I wrapped my arms around my mom and held her tight. But I was undone and intently focused on the math. With the numbers not adding up, and the room now silent except for my father explaining their options in a calm monotone and controlled manner, like he was somehow in control of the situation, I couldn't take listening to him anymore. His words were shit. I bolted from the room, down the stairs of the split-level ranch, through the garage, and out to the sandy driveway. I was sobbing, shocked and in disbelief of the words I had just heard.

Just like that, whatever illusion I had been able to live, whatever fantasy overlay of my mother's life and my upbringing, it was gone. All colored by the death sentence my mother found herself living under the past few weeks of her life. Tragedy had never visited the Coleman family like this before. The country bumpkins had been blindsided by a Mack truck, wreckage splattered on the highway.

My mother was living a nightmare. And even by the time we had arrived that day, my father, who was gallivanting in blissful avoidance of reality, was living in denial. He went through the motions. He did what he was supposed to do. But par for the course of my father's life, he maintained a military calm in the heat of battle and regurgitated reason.

Benny's world, although he didn't know it yet, had just been brushed out of sight in one fell swoop. It ceased to exist. His world, which rested on the fulcrum of my own, would be taken out by the same mad fate.

And the world I'd made up, the one I believed was *real*, the one that had Grandma rocking sweet baby swaddled in a hand-knitted baby blanket in the rocking chair, looking lovingly down at her blessed grandchild in her arms…It had just been blown to fucking bits. Our family's circle of life, our joy, had just come to an uninvited, abrupt end.

Things, as they say, would never be the same again.

Chapter 2

LOOKS LIKE STORMY WEATHER

So. When *does* it happen? When do you change? When exactly do you hit the tipping point? When do you go from thinking "maybe there's something better" and maybe you should take up a hobby like perennial gardening or scrapbooking or Pilates to *"I gotta get the fuck out of here!"*? Can you ever see it coming, or are you doomed to have it happen all of a sudden, like standing on a sidewalk and having a piano land on top of you?

When?

When you're sitting crisscross-applesauce with your toddler at a play date and listening to one of the other mothers blabber on and on about a new, unnecessary toy she found at Walmart? Or how she's throwing target-practice goldfish crackers in the toilet to try and get her two-year-old to pee in the potty? One afternoon while staring into the freezer, wondering what to defrost for dinner? Or maybe while stirring the mac-n-cheese while simultaneously flipping the chicken nuggets, Dora the "Explora" singing in the background? In the middle of another exhausting, endless night changing yet another in a forever line of dirty diapers?

Or does it happen on a Tuesday evening as the kids run from room to room, and he arrives home at the end of his long day? When he gives you another dry, perfunctory kiss and, a second later, his lips start moving and some noise comes out, words maybe, about work maybe, but the words just don't add up to anything but static and noise. He's sure to be telling you something he thinks is important, but you realize you cannot bear to even try to listen; you can't even fake it anymore.

You hear words coming out, but you can't will yourself to even try to pay attention.

You just don't give a shit.

You think maybe you're having a nervous breakdown or a mini stroke; maybe it's senility of the personality-portion of your brain or something, because everything *feels* different. It's like everything you've ever known and believed in, everything you've ever held dear, has suddenly become strange and disturbing, and everything that's ever seemed distant and frightening suddenly looks intriguing and interesting. It *would* be cool to cancel Christmas this year, replacing our over commercialized holiday with a trip to the Caribbean. It *would* be exhilarating to read poetry out loud to each other, legs stretched out together on the bed. It *would* be markedly satisfying to tell that self-absorbed, boring mother at the mommy group to please do everyone a favor and just shut the fuck up.

You feel like the picture has blurred. Your senses are confused. You feel like the warm and cool air outside no longer run together to make a pleasant breeze but now they've turned course, moving in different directions, creating a storm up there somewhere, and making you feel hot and cold all at once.

There's a crisis looming, and you realize that you don't have enough time to get out of the way. All the dodges, all the fakes, all the excuses that have served you so well over the months and years of your life are guaranteed to fail you. Yes, you can see it coming, but you can't make yourself turn away, like staring at a horrible car crash on the highway. At that moment you realize that you are powerless to stop it. That moment. It's then. You freeze when you realize that you've got nothing. Your inborn defenses have run dry. The tricks you've learned along the way are useless. You might just as well be standing naked up on the gym stage in front of your high school class fumbling to recite Shakespeare, wondering why you hadn't shaved your legs.

Your legs. They feel like maybe they might just give way. Your senses are both dulled and heightened at the same time. There's a

Recipe for Disaster

lump in your throat. You wonder—was that the loudest thunder you'd ever heard, or was it just a plane flying real low overhead? Did anyone else hear that? Maybe a truck rumbling along the road? You can't hear a word he's saying to you, but you hear the cartoon people blathering incessantly on the television; you can hear a lone dog baying somewhere down the road.

You can't smell his breath and scent anymore, a smell you once found attractive—it's been replaced by the smell of your own fear.

You clench up. You've got to get through this moment. Get a grip. Pray that maybe it was nothing of note. Something you ate upset you. A virus coming on. Maybe that panic in your belly was just that, a momentary panic. Maybe it'll pass. After all, it's passed before. Breathe. Just breathe. Everything will be all right. You've just got to breathe your way through it. Close your eyes. Relax your shoulders. Breathe in through your nose, out through your mouth. Unclench your hands. Picture a field filled with beautiful flowers. Breathe. Just like they told you in that Lamaze class when you were pregnant. Breathe.

Only God knows what you're trying to birth now.

Just breathe.

Yes, that's it. Settle it down. Keep mashing the ground meat. Add an egg. Bread crumbs. Some ketchup. Salt and pepper. Keep nodding your head as his lips move. Smile. "Wow, you're kidding. I can't believe that. No wonder you're tired." Tilt your head to the left just a tad. Don your understanding expression. Raise the eyebrows a little. Tell him it'll all work out, always does.

Newly married women can feign ignorance about what I'm saying. But if you've been married more than a few years and you say you don't know what I'm talking about, I have to respectfully say you're either a liar or deader than the four-day-old meatloaf in the back of the fridge. It happens! You can't help it. She gets bored. He gets boring. Or he gets bored. She gets boring. Things change.

For those of you who really have no idea what I'm talking about—I envy you. I'm jealous of you and happy for you at the same time. You married your high school sweetheart and are still best friends to this day. I wish I'd been you. I wish I never found myself staring into that dark abyss. I didn't want this to happen to my life. For years, I fought it hard, feet planted firmly into the grounding of my picture-perfect life. Determined to make it work, to force the feelings, to ignore the storm, to keep mixing the meatloaf and loving my handed-down life.

But eventually, I lost. She won. She? Yes, she. The person I had ignored for twenty-six years. She cried out. She cried "Uncle." Fucking I-can't-stand-this-is-happening uncle.

With no money, enough debt to make even a rational person jump the bridge, a worn-down, frail-at-best emotional foundation, and two precious children with tears of confusion in their eyes—I ran the white flag up the flagpole. I couldn't live a lie anymore.

As bad as all that was, I knew for sure that the thing that would destroy me would be to pretend that what I now knew to be absolute truth was a lie. That would have been a crime against nature. *That's* what messes people up. You have to embrace the moment. Embrace the *honest*. It doesn't have to be the end of the world you've so carefully pieced together. It was for me, but if you are in love and you're smart and you're honest, you can actually make everything work out. It doesn't have to be the end—or the beginning of the end—of your world. But be honest enough to accept that it might be.

It just happened to be the end of that world for me.

I didn't want it to be.

I didn't mean it to be.

I was furious that it was.

I didn't mean to change. And I don't know where she came from. I didn't mean to become unhappy with the life I had dreamed about living from the time I was a little girl, for as long as I could remember. I didn't want to change. But I did. I was unhappy. Unhappy? No, there's an overused word. I was way more than "unhappy." I was…dissatisfied. I was confused. I was *unsettled*. I was like someone who'd embarked on a wondrous journey only to land in the wrong place.

How did this happen?

It wasn't supposed to be this way. I played by the rules. I was a good kid. Sure, I gave my parents a fair share of heartache and worry, but nothing out of the ordinary. I got my degree. I got married. We bought the right house. We had two perfect, beautiful children.

I did everything on the list of things that you're supposed to do to live a good, decent life. Check. Check. And, check.

I worked damned hard to get to this point. Both Ben and I did. College. Starting a career. Finding "love." Building a home. God, I wanted it all to happen so quickly. Hurry, hurry, hurry. And then, *whoa*! How'd I get here? Someone stop this merry-go-round and give me a minute to think. To plan. To ponder.

Maybe to get off.

Give me a minute to breathe.

A friend of mine, a guy who is very successful in all the ways you'd ever think to measure success—prominent attorney, wealthy, big house, nice cars, two cute-as-hell little girls—found out the hard way that getting off the merry-go-round isn't about money, isn't about the house, the car, or the reputation and the trophy wife.

"I gave her everything," he told me, arms crossed in his power stance, when he told me about losing her.

I wish I had had the strength to tell him, no, he didn't. He didn't give his wife the one thing she needed more than the house and the cars and the all-American dream. He didn't give her *herself*. All the things he gave her, all the things she *wanted*, had just made it harder and harder for her to find herself. And unfortunately, she'd never known to look for herself, either. She'd been a true believer, same as him. But then she'd lost her faith.

"She didn't have to work a day. Didn't have to lift a finger. There was a housekeeper. We had a nanny. She had it all."

He just kept adding one and one together and couldn't see how she'd come up with three. How the pretty woman he'd married, the one with the spa appointments and country club lunches, end up having a breakdown at thirty-seven and leaving him for her weight-lifting athletic trainer who drove a used Nissan?

"Out of nowhere," he said sadly.

Nowhere, you say?

Nowhere was a place I knew only too well. I *lived* there.

"What did she have to be unhappy about?" he asked me. "Name me one thing that she had to be unhappy and dissatisfied about."

Hmm. I'd have to get back to him on that.

Not that the moment comes out of nowhere. It never does. In retrospect, it's obvious. It's just that in the forward living of life, you don't see it coming. For me, there were signs I was going to have problems with the conventional life I was investing my dreams into, back from the age of twelve. But who had the insight or the smarts or the courage to read the signs then? I never knew I had a voice.

I just accepted that I should work on the simple recipe handed to me, because that's what was *supposed* to happen. That's what I was supposed to do.

There was a time in my life when I first heard the term "midlife crisis." All of a sudden, I started paying attention to the buzz about men having "midlife crises," when all these once-familiar men started sporting comb-overs or shaving their heads. You saw them driving the highway—shiny convertible, going eighty, with something like LVNCRZY on the license plate. Whispers surround them about a girlfriend, a secretary or an office assistant. Then there's the public divorce. An ugly divorce.

Why? Because after most of his life pushing himself to get to "where he was," he finally had time to look around at where he was and ask, "Am I happy?"

When I was younger, I thought those men were the "bad guys." They hadn't done what they were supposed to do. They didn't keep their end of the bargain. They were married. They had families. Lives. Responsibilities. Promises.

Now, I'm not so sure who are the good guys and who are the bad guys.

I'm the one who didn't keep her end of the bargain.

Now I believe that it isn't so easy. There is no good answer to that question, "Am I happy?" that will allow you to keep on doing what you've always done, without either changing or limping on, carrying some deep, psychic wound.

And now, more than not, it's the women who are stirring things up midlife. But they aren't all waiting for midlife. For some, it's when the kids are old enough to be independent. Then, they look around at the turned-upside-down house and wonder if there's more than washing and cleaning. Or even when their children are young: when they realize that the reality isn't the same as when they were little girls with their dolls "playing mommy."

We have so many opportunities and options that our mothers and grandmothers did not have. But we still make the same kinds of compromises and choices. We still buy into the same conventional dreams. We still internalize the same kinds of rules. We don't recognize that we have a voice.

Be a good girl.

Do your homework.

Do well in school.

Fall in love and marry (someone just like your dad).

Have kids.

And "happily ever after" will surely be yours.

Aaaaaaaagghhh! (That's the sound of me screaming.)

Chapter 3

EVERY OTHER THURSDAY

It was early October 2003. I was standing at the kitchen counter of our split-level ranch in upstate New York. There I stood, ten steps from the door leading to the attached garage that housed my brand-new SUV. Twenty steps from where Sara was taking her afternoon nap in her crib, unaware that her mother was about to snap. A mere four steps from the refrigerator—home to a twelve-pack of cold beer. Cold, frosty, inviting beer.

I was, in short, geographically and psychically, smack-frigging-dab in the middle of *My Recipe*, the recipe as my life would have it, in black and white on a 3x5 index card.

My mother, in remission a good year now from pancreatic cancer and the surgery that almost killed her, had just left from another weeklong visit. Since her recovery, for all intents and purposes, her cancer was gone! She had beaten the odds and now had moved on to more important things like spending time with Sara and making memories of a lifetime. Her strength and determination had astounded my sister and me—never did we dream this petite, soft-spoken woman would fight so hard to come back stronger than ever. She had taken a life-ending-size tumor and beaten it to a pulp. A little girl named Sara, her pot of gold at the end of the rainbow, kept her fighting. And she won. She won big time.

It was one of those perfect, crisp October afternoons. Cool but with the air so clear you could see the leaves in brilliant color, either hanging on to their twig or joyfully letting go and dancing to their resting place on the ground. It was getting a lot cooler as the sun began to hide behind the trees.

Mom had left that late morning after breakfast. Sara and I had lunch, then I put her down for her nap. Nothing much special about the day, a Thursday I'd lived before and would live again. I walked to the mailbox and brought in the mail and set it on the kitchen counter. And then I just stood there for a few moments and started thinking about what we would have for dinner. I turned and walked a few steps over to the sink and found myself staring out through the kitchen window into the growing darkness as the sun sunk too early behind the intruding trees. Then, my attention was drawn back to the counter, I found myself staring at the mail, at one envelope in particular.

I sighed heavily. There was no particular emotion in my exhale. My affect was merely flat. I recognized the envelope well. It was his paycheck.

Why, oh why didn't I ever learn to just leave well enough alone? Usually, whenever I opened his check every other Thursday, I did so with the completely irrational hope and anticipation that this one would be different, this one would have different numbers, numbers that would allow us to change our lives, to live easier, more comfortably, more happily. A little room to stretch, to have some fun maybe. Replace the dilapidated deck maybe. And each time, the numbers told the same story. Month to month. Year to year. This time wasn't any different. I knew it wouldn't be. I hoped and prayed it would be. But it wasn't. When I opened it, I could see there was no change. The numbers, as they say, don't lie. There was no change. Not from the last one or the one before that. Or before that or before that or before that.

Steady. Regular. Predictable. Like clockwork.

If anything, the numbers were shrinking a bit. Less overtime. Higher insurance. Such was the thanks due for the privilege of a secure and steady position as a law enforcement officer in the state of New York. Shouldn't a guy who wears a bullet-proof vest to work every day make more? I'd think to myself.

Steady and predictable wasn't cutting it any more.

Recipe for Disaster

Jesus H. Christ. We were sinking. I could feel it. Day by day. Week by week, we were losing ground. And Ben's check wasn't going to lift us up. Neither was my job working part-time as a nurse. Obviously, I made better money working full-time, but we'd agreed when Sara was born that I would cut back so I could be home with her as much as possible.

"Your being with her is more important than any amount of money. We don't want her in daycare full-time," Ben had said.

How noble.

Of course, he was right. What could I do but agree? There was nothing more important than a child being with her mother. Nurturing and guiding her was our highest priority.

All that. And there I was, in my kitchen on that October afternoon. I remember feeling like there was a quiet blanketing the afternoon sounds. You could hear voices somewhere outside, but you had no idea if they were nearby or far away, no idea if they were just kids playing or something menacing and snickering. There was a car driving on the road somewhere. Was it coming closer or driving away? Did it want me to hop in? Slowly, I glanced around the kitchen, my kitchen, and took a look at my house. It seemed to me that I was seeing it for the first time. Whatever charm I had ever assigned to it seemed to have evaporated. Whatever had made it singular and special was gone. In the place of *my* house, I saw a dated, boxed-out structure. Each room divided by walls. No open space to speak of. Low, confining ceilings. Smothering.

Only my eyes moved as I took in my surroundings.

To the side of the sink, there were my mother's bequeathed Betty Croker and baby food cookbooks. To the left, coffee stains on the microwave that I'd wiped a thousand times but could never get off. Straight ahead, the salt-and-pepper-shakers-combo-napkin set centered perfectly on the oak table, one of many furniture pieces gifted to us from his parents.

It was all so nice, all so rational, all so my mother and father, all so…so…suffocating.

This was our first house. We'd saved every penny to buy it. Even so, we could barely afford it. Almost everything in it was either a gift or a hand-me-down. We'd worked hard to make it nice, to make it home. We planted flowers in the garden. We painted the walls. Put up new curtains. A new light fixture. We fixed things up.

I liked our home.

I felt comfortable enough there.

But I would be lying if I said I didn't feel isolated there as well. Secluded. Cut off. Like everything I really wanted in life was just past my reach. Just down the road a bit. That way.

Like I was on the outside looking in.

And then, like a burst of wind entering the room, I felt a kind of panic grip my throat. I braced both my hands on the sides of the sink and stared out the window, straining to see into the deepening woods. At first, it was hard to see past my own reflection in the darkening glass. But then I could see past myself to the outlines of the trees and foliage in the back of the house.

Some leaves whipped through the air, caught up on the breeze. They scraped against the window and then flew off. So many leaves. Our backyard abutted some woods, so there were trees so deep you couldn't see the end of them even in the middle of the afternoon. Sometimes I felt like those trees were moving closer and closer to the house, closing in on me. A branch around my throat. Leaves tumbling into my eyes, scratching my face.

Among his many other skills and talents, Ben is an arborist, and he takes great pride in the trees and the garden. I don't know if it was just a coincidence, but he seemed to have been expert in all the things I had come to find suffocating.

Me…I had begged him over and over, "Please cut some of those goddamn trees down. Let in some air! Let in some light!"

He replied in a tone implying I was some kind of an idiot, "You can't just cut down trees randomly. Trees are in stages. They work together. The trees are just fine there." He shook his head. "I would hate it if you could see a neighbor's house there. With the trees, it's like no one else is around, and it helps keep the car noise down."

Yeah. Great. Five fucking cars drive by our house every day. I wasn't worried about a neighbor's house being close. I *needed* something, someone, to be close.

When it came to trees, like everything else, he was in charge. He was the one to decide how many and how tall, what kind and when to prune them. He was in control.

"Just cut the things down and make some room so I can breathe!" I wanted to shout at him. "There's nothing back there but woods! Woods and woods and woods." But I didn't. I kept quiet, letting the sense of those trees creeping closer and closer just keep growing in me. Hoping that maybe one day I would fall in love with them the same way he was.

I started to pace for a minute. Back and forth. Back and forth. I sat at the counter a moment. Up again. I returned to the window and started to drum my fingers on the circa-1986 I-threw-up-country-blue countertop. I knew that this time, something would have to give. Something was *gonna* give. When I couldn't stand the noise of my fingers drumming on the counter, I dropped my elbows to the counter and cupped my face in my hands.

What's that feeling in my throat? Something is choking me.

What was I going to do?

About what? I knew I had to do something, but I didn't quite know about what! Something was bugging me, something deep. But I couldn't quite put my finger on what it was. Like an itch I couldn't quite reach, I felt irked and irritated, nervous and unsettled.

I couldn't sort out what I was trying to sort out, and that was bugging the shit out of me.

I saw Ben's check on the counter. I looked around the kitchen again, and throughout the dining room.

And then…It hit me.

I could move the furniture around till the cows came home. We could paint the rooms, and I could hang new decorative bordering. We could cut down some trees or plant more flowers. But *fundamentally* nothing was ever going to magically change. This was it. This was our life.

We would live paycheck to paycheck for the rest of our lives. This piece of paper on the kitchen counter represented opportunity in our lives. We would eke out our existence and measure it with tax bills, 70-percent-off holiday decorations at the dollar store, Hallmark sentiments, and a deepening void between us.

Most disturbing of all, I realized that that was *exactly as my recipe for my life would have it*. It was the life my parents lived. A life I'd been quite ready to live, to embrace. A good life. A decent life. A conventional life. I had chosen a career, a good career, a respectable career, but a career with limited potential. I had married a man, a good man, a decent man, but a man who was a lifetime subscriber to the unending, unchanging edition of *The Status Quo*.

I had set the inertia of my life in motion, and in motion it would continue—unless something happened. Unless something acted on my life to change it. "Please God, *do* something!" Couldn't I move to Barbados and lives my days with nothing but the sand, a tan, and good books? Couldn't Leonardo DiCaprio's car break down outside the house, and realizing immediately upon seeing me that he must whisk me off with him? Couldn't a random attorney from Ohio call and tell me the great-aunt I never knew has left a college-saving inheritance for Sara?

But I knew those things would never happen. Get your head out of your ass, Melissa.

If anything was going to change in my life, *I* would have to be the agent of that change. *I* would have to alter the recipe and stir things up.

It was only then, on this random Thursday, that I truly appreciated how "late to the dinner table" of my life I was.

With that revelation—that I was the only one who could do anything about my life—I was jarred into action. Unfocused, desperate, and with urgency, I rushed down to the family room and fired up the computer. I might not have a clue about how to change my life but dammit, the Internet would have something for me.

I opened Google and quickly typed in: "How to make money from home."

Recipe for Disaster

I felt a glow of satisfaction as thousands upon thousands of results showed up in some ridiculously, unthinkable fraction of a second.

Medical transcriptionist. OK, I could do that, but why would I? It's such a step backward...I'd have to take a class and then...Is there really anything more boring than sitting around on my ass all day pounding a keyboard transcribing doctors' notes? Not for me.

Wait! I thought, glancing away from the screen—what about waitressing? It's not from home, but there's something I could do with ease. I could always go back to schlepping tables. With a friendly smile and some easy banter, I'd always done well with tips. Oh wait, then who would watch Sara when Ben worked evenings? No, my life couldn't accommodate waitressing.

Selling online? Homemade jewelry? Stuffing envelopes? Telemarketer? Avon? Massage therapist? Umm, *no*! Touching people I don't know and rubbing them down...yuck. Scratch that.

After thirty minutes of pounding away at the mouse and keyboard, I sat there staring at the computer screen, demoralized and deflated. Google—infinitely wise, infinitely fast, infinitely knowing Google—what happened? I must have thought that the World Wide Web would answer my prayers, like some beneficent God. But no. The computer just spewed out random information for me to sift through. There was no wisdom. No guidance. No flashing neon sign saying "You've found it, Melissa!" Actually, not even a glimmer of hope.

I was in dire straits, in desperate need of salvation. I felt myself teetering on a precipice of an invisible crossroads. I didn't ask for this to happen today. Why now? Why my life?

But the revelation of what had become clear to me that day had placed before me a storm.

There I was, sitting in silence, covered in the warm glow of computer screen light. Seven steps away from the back door leading to the outside world. Eight steps from Sara's toys, which I still hadn't picked up from the living room floor. A mere twenty steps from the comforting, frosty ones in the refrigerator.

Such was the landscape of my life, of my world. And I felt it closing in. Shrinking in on me. What was I going to do?

Just when I thought I would cry in frustration, I heard the *rattle, rattle* of Sara pulling on the crib rail. Unbidden, a smile came to my lips. I was released. My purpose was clear. My post-colicky cherub was awake from her nap!

I was the mommy.

Up the two flights to her room, I jetted, opened the door to her room, and was greeted by her contagious smile that warmed me like summer sunshine, her crinkly nose hiding behind the pacifier. These were moments that filled me with a sense of perfection and joy. Upon waking up from her naps, she was always excited and happy to see me. She jumped up and down with the thrill of the door opening, rattling the crib even more.

"Hi, honey. How was your nappy?" I asked warmly as I swept her up in my arms. "How 'bout we leave The Binks in your bed with your friends?"

Without hesitation, Sara grabbed the binky and threw it down to her crib, where it bounced off her dolly du jour and stuffed doggie. A move she always made with a proud satisfaction. She wrapped her legs around me and hugged me tight. My little girl, so warm and snuggly, safe in my arms. Love.

Off we went to the kitchen for a sippy cup and snack!

The exhaustion of Sara's colicky period was a dim memory. She was sleeping well and was a true joy for both Ben and me. My days with her at home were peaceful and sweet. My mother would visit frequently and spend a week at a time with Sara, playing with and loving her. We passed the time watching *Barney* and *Charlotte's Web*, dancing to music, playing make-believe, picking berries, and going for walks to explore. She found intrigue and excitement in grasshoppers and trickling streams.

When I was with her then, my recipe made sense. When I was with her, I loved my recipe. My life was meaningful and certain.

It was true. As if by magic, hearing Sara awaken in her crib transported me back to a sense of purpose and goodness. I was happily and gratefully transported back. The lack of money, or more appropriately, opportunity, was already a distant memory, like the far-off rumbling of a storm that has come and gone and moved on over the hills to the next county.

Distant, but a memory nonetheless. The discontent had subsided, but it hadn't disappeared. One more meal, solid and predictable, but one that only temporarily satisfied. With Sara in my arms and a beautiful late afternoon to explore, my life was good.

Decent is acceptable.

Conventional is good.

This was my life. This was what I *wanted*. With Sara by my side, it was exactly what I'd "signed up for." I couldn't even imagine how to conceive, let alone live, a different life. I wasn't a Stepford wife by any stretch. If you had asked me then, I would have said I was happy. Happily married. Happy with my marriage. My baby. My life. Happy. Yes, happy. Why do you ask?

But I wasn't.

I wasn't even me. The real Melissa had only begun to make her presence known, to peek out from deep inside my psyche. And from my first glimpse of her, I was scared of her. She was like a bully waiting for me inside the girls' bathroom in sixth grade. She made me want to stay hidden in my room with a terminal illness. I wanted her to go away and to stay away. I wanted to be able to believe that my life was fine, just fine.

And it *was*. It was fine.

Just. Fine.

Nothing more, nothing less. I don't know when it happened, but I'd become like Goldilocks in the story that my mother used to read to Sara. I had opted out of the too-big and the too-small, the too-hot and the too-cold. I had embraced the "just right."

But what I realized was that it wasn't the "just right" that I'd found. I'd found tepid and uninspired.

I'd found the land of normal.

And the real Melissa was lurking. A roaring thunder was looming. The time was limited.

And I wasn't gonna last here at all.

Chapter 4
CHANNEL SURFING

I had become my mother. I felt like I had taken her housecoat and slipped it on. While it was incredibly comfortable and *comforting* to have her presence so close to me—to be able to breathe in her smell—it turned my heart barren to realize just how well the old housecoat actually fit me.

We look at things, at our material lives, and measure where we are in life. Have we "made" it? Are we "losing ground"? How come our neighbor can afford a new Audi, and we're still driving a twelve-year-old Toyota?

I considered that I must be spoiled and shallow. Materialistic, never satisfied. There were lots of times during that October stretch when I said to myself, "Just wake up, Melissa. Suck it up and live your life. What are you complaining about?" God, there was a part of me that wanted to do just that: to just wake up and quit "complaining." I had a good life. A decent life. A life that a lot of people would envy. Isn't this the goddamn life we strive for?

I had a nice house. Not a mansion, but a nice, middle-class, comfy house. Why did I want to cry all the time then? My physical surroundings were not the point, though. I focused on them because they mirrored what was going on inside me. My house felt confining not because it was small, or because of the walls, or the trees. It felt confining because it was, for the most part, exactly the same house I had grown up in: a split-level ranch for my split-level life. Where the hell was the woman I was supposed to grow up to be?

Hell, my life was a mirror image of my mother's life. I couldn't look in the mirror without seeing my mother—and not just a physical resemblance to my mother, but I also saw all that my mother never was and what she could have been; I saw the sadness in her eyes that I never acknowledged. Like there was a story there that would never be told.

I saw the shrunken boundaries of her life imposed upon my own.

The same constraints that limited my mother were limiting me: self-imposed resignation, turf conceded, decisions deferred.

When I looked in the mirror, instead of her smiling face, I saw the desperation in her eyes, the desperation that had made me feel vulnerable as a girl, the desperation that made me feel that she would have done almost anything to break free of her life. A woman married to a man who had a say in all matters of the house and home.

But she didn't. She did what she was supposed to. She was a good girl.

Like her, I did what I was "supposed to do." I always had. I don't know if I even believed that there was another way. Like seeing and naming a new color, I couldn't imagine another way if I tried. As a consequence, each day my own voice, my own personality, my hope for getting to know the "real Melissa" diminished.

The "real Melissa" was my enemy because just by existing, she made it clear I was unhappy and becoming a crappy liar to boot.

Understand, my internal drama was not Ben's fault. Whatever ended up throwing me for a loop threw him for a loop too. But, we became like oil and water. Maybe I'm lucky that I "broke" first. One of us had to. Maybe he was just too patient, too disciplined, too grounded, too committed to be the one.

He, like me I'm sure, couldn't even fathom the idea that the life we had created wasn't going to work.

That didn't mean that it was easy.

Ben wasn't so much rigid as set and comfortable with his expectations and his vision of what our life should be. Because I was neither set nor comfortable, I ceded just about everything to his vision.

There wasn't much I could do inside or outside the house, inside or outside my own home, without Ben's approval. There was no plant planted, rosebush pruned, room painted, piece of furniture arranged that wasn't OK'd by Ben. Nothing was purchased. No rug was laid down. No lighting fixture was replaced. No holiday dinner was cooked. No wallpaper stripped. No electronic purchased. Not one thing, large or medium, was done without Benny's approval.

I longed for the freedom and independence to manage the home without being micromanaged. I get that men want to have control over big projects. I understand that adding a room or putting in a new faucet is a "man's" thing. But why would I have to have Ben's approval for a new toaster oven? Why did he have to have something negative to say about new curtains, or a lamp, or rearranging the fucking couch?

(He also hated when I swore. Fucking drove him nuts.)

"Why do we need that?" he'd ask, slightly insultingly. What he really meant was "I didn't say that was OK."

A new shower curtain. A bed comforter. A toy for Sara. I could feel him judging my decisions, watching my moves.

It was like being in a living, three-dimensional chess game, and I was being checkmated at every turn.

I shouldn't have been surprised. When we were registering for our wedding, Ben was adamant about every aspect of our registry planning. He insisted on having the final say about our dishes and our silverware. At the time, I thought it was crazy but crazy in a good way.

"Look at me," I had thought to myself, "I have a caring guy who actually really, really cares about the pattern of our dish set. How lucky am I?"

The problem with controlling guys is that even when they are good, even when they are caring and decent, even when their decisions are true, they cannot help but stunt you. It's not that they mean to. They can't help it. It is not enough for them to win the chess game. They have to win each and every move. You have no freedom on the board. You can't move left or right without their say-so. Over time, you become timid. You second-guess every decision you make, even what you're wearing. Even the makeup you put on and the dresses you wear.

The traits that made him such a good cop weren't something he could just leave at work. He couldn't make the transition from being the kind of man who was a good cop at work to being a good man at home. And if he couldn't do that, if he couldn't be "just the husband" at home, I couldn't be "just the wife." I'm always some version of a potential criminal, someone whose every move has to be carefully monitored and controlled. No situation, no moment, can escape his control.

And it seemed the less control he was able to wrangle at work, as things worsened with the state of affairs at his job, the more control he sought at home.

I learned early on to consult Ben about everything. If I didn't, there would be emotional fallout. He was clear about what he wanted and expected, and I, being a good girl, was anything but clear about what I wanted or expected. And then, when that light fixture tarnished, the electronic thingy-gingy broke or didn't toast the toast correctly, or the wallpaper started to peel—it'd get thrown in my face. Because, most certainly, it was my fault.

My life was a process of clearing my choices through judge and jury first.

I don't think Ben ever had any idea who I really was. How could he? I barely knew. And when I was starting to figure it out, I couldn't talk to him. His way taught me to be cautious around him, to hide my real self. When Ben was in the house, I felt I was always walking on eggshells. When he was around, and even when he wasn't, everything I did was measured up against what he thought and what he deemed good and acceptable.

And so this went on for a few years, the role and dance of husband and wife, controller and controlled.

But, like a timid deer crossing a six-lane highway at rush hour, eventually, I didn't have a fucking prayer.

I have a friend who is locked into an emotionless, loveless marriage. He's mostly just frustrated by how his wife is continually doing projects around the house—a wall taken down for a new pantry in the kitchen, fixtures replaced in the bathroom, fresh painting, seasonal decorating. She buys candles, wall hangings, candelabras, and picture frames. She buys shit for bookcases and mantels and ten things the kids don't need that week.

"I don't know why she doesn't get it. Why she can't just let things be," he said to me one day.

I looked at him. "You want my opinion?"

He looked at me curiously, like he wasn't sure. "OK," he said after a moment, clearly not convinced he really wanted to hear what I thought.

I drew a deep breath. By giving my opinion, I knew I was revealing a lesson learned the hard way. I was giving up a piece of myself. "Inside, she thinks that if she changes things in the house, her surroundings, she will fix things in your relationship and within herself. And it will make her feel better."

He looked at me. The tiniest sliver of a smirk appeared on the left side of his mouth, as if he knew that he already knew this but had not verbalized it. He knew it. He'd just never let that knowledge break to the surface.

I shook my head. "But it won't work," I said flatly. "She can change every room in the fricking house for the next ten years, and it won't make any difference. She is not happy. The renovation project is on the inside." I shrugged. "A much more difficult and costly task."

He was thoughtful after I said that, but no more thoughtful than I was. I knew only too well how his wife felt. I had gotten to the point where I couldn't go into any room of our house without finding things I wanted to change. Constantly my mind would lean down that road. The rug needed to be pulled up, those curtains needed to be changed out for the other ones, that picture frame should be centered on the shelf more, and the other picture needed to be moved three inches to the right, that basket of toys moved kitty-corner, and on the other side of the room, I wanted the rocking chair here. No, there. Wait—maybe it was best where it was? Room to room I would wander, for hours sometimes, rearranging random articles to create a new, fresh feel. A change!

The entire house needed renovating.

Which was to say, I needed renovating.

But I couldn't even go through the ghost motions of changing larger things in the house without Ben saying it was OK. So I eventually became a master of changing the little things, the barely noticeable things, making tiny changes one at a time, gradually. Changes so small, he never even noticed.

Until it was too late.

No room in the house was as unsatisfying to me as our bedroom. The carpet in our bedroom was decades old. It hadn't been replaced since the house was built. Not only had it seen more than its share of wear and tear, it was musty, dirty, and ca-ca brown with animal pee stains.

That old shag made me feel like I was in a time warp of someone else's life every time I set foot in there. But it wasn't only the carpet that threw me into a time warp. Our bedroom furniture was made up of mismatched pieces from various antiques that his parents had kindly given to us. I hated that furniture. Not that I was in a position to turn away their kindness in giving it to us. We needed the furniture, and we didn't have the money to buy new furniture when we moved into the house, but goddammit, each time I opened one of the drawers to the dresser and the drawer bottom fell out, I couldn't help but swear under my breath.

Still, I knew I should consider myself lucky we had a dresser at all. It wouldn't have mattered to Benny if we kept our clothes in milk crates stacked against the wall or if our bed was just a mattress on the floor.

But like my friend's wife in her loveless marriage, it wasn't the room that I was dissatisfied with. It was me and my powerlessness to redecorate it. I never really knew who I was there, who the person who slept there was. I could not walk through the door of my own bedroom without shaking my head and thinking, "This bears absolutely no resemblance to the bedroom I wanted as an adult. None at all."

And yet, there I was, an adult, and that was the bedroom where I slept.

My bedroom.

I was a stranger there, but I felt helpless to change the room or myself. There were set "rules" about what I could and could not do. They were, for the most part, unwritten, and because they were unwritten, they were more restrictive and they made me feel off-balance, uncertain, unsure.

Timid.

If Ben felt the same way, I sure as hell didn't know it. He was very clear about what he thought belonged in the bedroom and what didn't. In his mind, the bedroom should be focused on two things. Anything that detracted from those things was forbidden.

Therefore, Benny refused to have a television in the bedroom.

"I won't allow one in there," he said. "I know what happens when people lay in bed watching TV. Soon, people just watch the television and forget about each other."

"But it's relaxing," I protested.

"The couch is for relaxing."

"Even if you wanted to watch college hoops with me? We could channel surf!"

He laughed. "I'll watch in the living room."

"Sweet sixteen?" I teased.

"I'll give you a sweet sixteen," he teased back, giving me a brief glimpse of the Benny I fell in love with.

We had this conversation, and lots more like it in all sorts of variations, while we lay in bed. We were young parents. We were still practically newlyweds.

Everyone works through this kind of stuff.

His presence told me everything would be fine. He was strong, and he knew what was best. So I was disturbed and confused when, before long, a part of me started to recoil in the evenings.

I was like a subject in some warped version of a Pavlov experiment. The more Benny wanted to get close, the less I wanted his closeness. I was being "trained" to be less so.

Maybe the double standard of his judgment had something to do with that. We couldn't have a television in the bedroom because it took away from our intimacy, but he didn't think that the *Time* magazine he schlepped to bed each night was a problem. Nothing was better to rev up the old love engine like an editorial about wars in distant lands, a new killer bacteria, or political strife at home!

Some people can't fall asleep without the sound of Jay Leno's voice. Benny seemed unable to sleep without the sweet lullaby of the *Time* stories in his head.

Gag me.

I didn't understand the argument about the television but came to accept it. But his rule against Sara being brought into the bed with us, even on her fussiest nights, really pissed me off. According to him, her presence was sure to interfere with the two purposes of the bedroom. Therefore, she could not be brought in, and co-sleeping would royally make him angry.

"But just tonight so we can get some sleep. I'm so tired. I think she has a fever, and she's so fussy," I would plead, too exhausted to either fight or to give in.

He'd get so angry he'd bolt up at 4 a.m., storm out of the room, and move to the couch. In his world, co-snuggling and co-sleeping had no place in our bed. So, no television. No Sara. When she fussed or cried, I'd lay on the floor in her room, or sometimes fall asleep with her sitting up on the couch, or sometimes get her back into her crib to sleep. Then I would make my way back to our room, where I would collapse in exhaustion.

Over time, eventually, the "intimacy" I created for myself was hopping in bed in the evening with a good book. I'd create my own little world of comfort to fall asleep. Something, anything, to take my mind away. Any book that would open my world and mind up to the world beyond my small-town life. I read and absorbed nonfiction. I had enough make-believe in my own life. I longed for an escape *to* reality.

Benny was earnest, sometimes charming, and often determined to keep the love alive through the exhausting nights with a colicky baby after his own long hours at work and my being whipped from working and taking care of Sara. It was just that, for all his efforts, we seemed to be moving in opposite directions.

I started going to bed early, not long after putting Sara down. We're talking early—8:00, 8:30 p.m. He would come into the bedroom and kiss me goodnight but then retreat to the living room, still so wound up from his day that he wouldn't be able to sleep until much later after decompressing and channel surfing in front of the TV.

Was I really tired? Or was it boredom and an unconscious desire to avoid him? He would stay up and watch a cooking show on TV. Maybe he was right that a television in the bedroom would get in the way of our relationship, but if he was watching television in the living room while I was in the bedroom, then it was a guarantee that we'd be apart.

Sometimes, I could hear the television, and I would wish I were watching it with him. But I couldn't bring myself to go downstairs and join him.

"Can't we just have a television in the bedroom?" I'd ask him again and again. "It'd be fun. We'd watch together."

He'd shake his head. "No, I've got to stand my ground. It's not the place for it."

OK then. Fuck you. Why and how is it that you get the final say in this? Oh yeah, because I'm a good wife and abide by the rules of the household. The rules of my life.

So, chicken versus egg? Which came first? Was it his refusal to even try something that we could have enjoyed together that instead kept us from growing closer, or was it our growing apart that made us not want to do enjoyable things together?

We had been married for only four years. Practically newlyweds. Yet he'd become rigid and a bore. I'd become cold and a bitch.

Or was he always rigid and boring, and had I always been cold and bitchy? Christ, who can say which came first? All I know is that our ever-duller routine was a symptom of something terrible, an omen of a disaster looming.

Neither one of us was happy. We just didn't know *how* unhappy we were, and if we did, we couldn't bear to admit it to ourselves. Not yet.

Doing that would betray something fundamentally false in us, something that felt worse than the lie itself.

Neither of us was prepared for that. Not yet. Maybe not ever. How do you prepare for the revelation that your marriage is an unauthentic imposter, pristinely disguised, but yet a lie?

Chapter 5

BASKET CASE

Our time with Sara was blissful now. Words cannot describe the joy she brought. Mommyhood fit me well. But, TV-less bedrooms, a boring marriage, meat and potatoes for dinner—there was a storm rumbling on the other side of the western hills.

One evening, I had gone to bed early as usual. I read for a bit but wasn't tired, and I didn't fall asleep. I was lying there, staring up at the ceiling, when I turned my head at the sound of Ben's footsteps.

"You asleep?" he asked softly.

I shook my head. "Sort of."

"I checked in on Sara. She's out."

I smiled to myself, envisioning the position I knew she was in, with her arms above her head, making little sucks on her binky while she dreamt peaceful baby-dreams. He always checked in to make sure Sara and I were OK. "That's good. I love her so much," I said.

He came closer to the bed. "I'll be up a bit later," he said.

I nodded. I had no idea what "a bit later" meant. It was always my goal to be asleep before he came up to go to bed. A score of another day's status post: no intimacy.

He leaned over and kissed me. "Good night," he said, just like he did every night. There was sweetness to Ben's ritual attentiveness. Like it was his duty as husband to tuck me in and say good night.

"You too," I said.

He straightened up and went to leave the room, attempting to pull the door closed. As always, I pleaded for him to leave it open. I couldn't stand to be in that room with the door closed. In the quiet after he left, my thoughts drifted. Slowly, I started to sink into that foggy place right between wakefulness and sleep, the place where thoughts get murky. Where the colors of the day get drained and start to float and swirl in the mind. Wakefulness seeps into sleep and sleep into wakefulness. Slowly, the unconscious starts to rouse. It's time for the mind to play tricks, for the disjointed thoughts to take stage.

Beyond the door, I could hear voices on the television. A famous cook was praising some other "fantastic dish": "Bam!" I tried to concentrate on what he was saying, but the words floated just beyond my consciousness. Words disappeared and were replaced by images.

Was I more asleep or more awake at that point? I could not say. The clouds of awake and asleep began to mix. Just then, a container… a basket of sorts appeared in my thoughts. There were pockets on the basket. A handle. And a lid. Not quite a picnic basket but similar to it. But there wasn't food in it. There were diapering things. All the stuff I had strewn out over the coffee table and the side table in the living room.

Suddenly, the baby paraphernalia that littered our house—from the living room to the kitchen counter and the nursery—swirled around, caught up in an eddy of my imagination. And then, swoosh, all the things that were strewn over the coffee table and floor fit perfectly into the basket, leaving the house neat and tidy.

My eyes opened wide.

Suddenly, I was wide awake.

That was cool, I thought. We could use one of those for Sara's diaper changes.

The basket, a vague image just a moment earlier, was now clear in my conscious mind.

"Real cool."

So cool that I had to do something about it. I sprang from the bed and went downstairs. As I passed the living room, Benny looked up.

"You OK?"

"Yeah, just gotta do something," I said as I hurried to the computer. I didn't need the computer though. What I needed was paper.

I grabbed a piece of paper from the printer and a pen and then went back upstairs.

Wide awake, I started to write and to sketch various versions of the basket, each with arrows pointing to the functional parts, accompanied by notes explaining each. I sat up in bed for about a half hour, elaborating on this basic idea that had hatched in my imagination and making it real by putting it on the page.

When I'd drained the idea from my head and drawn and labeled everything I could think of, I put the paper and notebook on my side table and turned off my light. Then I rested my head back down on the pillow and got into my sleeping position, my back facing the center of the bed. I wasn't sure what had just happened. I'd never really done something like that before. All I knew was that I was pleased I'd stayed awake to do what I'd just done. I felt a creative satisfaction I hadn't felt in a long time.

That said, I had no idea what I'd done or what it meant.

Not a goddamn clue to the extent of what had just been born.

Nothing, of course, grows in a vacuum. Even the wallop of initial insight and creativity incubates for a long time. Sometimes we're aware of that incubation. Sometimes it sneaks up on us, like those straws added one after the other to the camel's back until finally, a straw, a single straw that weighs no more than a feather, is the one that tips the balance, the one that brings down the camel.

That changes everything.

My moment of revelation was not the *end* but the beginning of what was to come next. The next step was innocuous enough, a failed shopping outing. All I needed was a diaper basket. A caddy-like thing. No biggie, right? When I left the house, I figured I'd run out and grab one.

"Really?" I said to the salesgirl. "Not even in the back? It's just like a basket, a container, you know…to hold the baby stuff."

"I'm sure," she said, politely.

After coming up dry at the next two stores, I couldn't believe it. These were three stores that *should have had* exactly what I was looking for. But they didn't. The stores carried diapers. Baby clothes. Creams. Baby thermometers. Burp cloths. Everything for the baby. But not the thing to carry it all in?

Perplexed, I wasn't about to be done in by lack of inventory. So when I was driving home from the stores, I told myself that I'd try to make one myself. I had to. I still needed a storage container for the baby-care stuff, after all.

So when I got home, I found my grandmother's 1950s Singer sewing machine in the basement and set it on the kitchen table in front of me. I stared at it like it was some alien creature. It might as well have been. My mom had taught me how to sew with that machine when I was a young girl, fascinated with how she could make clothes form out of cuts of fabric.

What little I had learned about sewing was difficult to remember. Feeding the bobbin and threading the needle, I started examining liners in other baskets and sewing my own liner together to fit a basket.

A few days later, just when I started to feel comfortable with my sewing, the machine stopped. More like froze up, and I knew it wasn't good. It was like a work animal that had finally had enough and stops in the middle of the field. Jammed. Busted. The scent of a little burning. I sat there and almost cried. I was sure that I was on to something. I rested my head on the table and closed my eyes. Shit.

What the hell was I going to do now?

I don't know where my determination came from. Maybe it wasn't determination at all, just desperation. Maybe that's the real understanding, that anyone who does anything new or different does it because he or she *has to*. They may have to in order to solve a particular problem, or they may have to because they are absolutely convinced that doing so will change their lives, or they may have to for a million different reasons.

And I had to make this diaper caddy. So no broken antique sewing machine was going to stop me.

By the end of the week, I had bought a new Singer and enrolled in a sewing class. I promised myself that I would make that sewing machine dance.

Before long, I had my pattern, prototype, and the first-round liner perfected and mapped out, and I knew how to keep making them. The pattern was sized exactly to fit into the standard basket that I had found at Basketville.

It was then I thought: "How could I sell these?"

Anyone can think of something and make it. That's just the start. The real challenge is taking that thing that you've made and making it a success—get it into the hands of all the people who might use it.

And that's what I intended to do. So, within the confines of my sheltered mind, I did what I thought everyone who wants to sell a product did...I set up a website and advertised on Google. Then I just waited for the orders to come in. (Ha, ha, ha!!! That is God (or maybe Google) laughing. Silly, silly, stupid girl!)

Good thing I didn't hold my breath. After weeks dabbling and fumbling with setting up my first online store, it went live. The SaraBear Diaper Caddy was officially born. Day one: no orders. Day two: no orders. Day three: a few hits from India, Somalia, and Who-the-hell-knows-ia...but no orders. Yeesh. Nothing came in except for charges from Google. No one called. No one emailed. No one inquired. Maybe the rest of the world went to a store where the shelves were always fully stocked with diaper caddies. Who knows?

But I hung in there. I spent way more money than I had to spend on Google advertising, but what were my other options? And it was then, during those first few weeks as I woke up daily to check the hits on the Adwords campaign, that I became addicted. Outright obsessed with selling this thing.

Slowly but surely, over the next months, orders started coming in. As they did, I'd make the caddies, my hands and knees on the family room floor, cutting and arranging. Sewing at 2 a.m. One by one, matching each to the order. I shipped to Texas, to California, and even tried shipping some to Canada. I would package the caddy in a cardboard box and ship it out from the post office.

I'd like to say that I enjoyed every moment of this hard-fought success, that each caddy I sewed and shipped was a vindication of the real

Melissa. But it would be a lie. The truth was I *hated* the entire process. There was not one part of it, not one step, that I found enjoyable or enriching. It sucked: every bit of it.

A sensible person would have thrown up her hands and said, "Fuck it. I tried. I've got to get focused on life and what to feed the kids for dinner."

Entrepreneurs are *not* sensible people. And, in something of a revelation to me, it turned out that I was becoming an entrepreneur. She'd been hiding.

The more I hated it, the more frustrating it was, the more I kicked myself, the more determined I was to figure out why it was frustrating, why I hated it, why I was kicking myself. And as soon as I figured that out, I was going to change it so I could create a successful business.

Every time a voice inside me said to give it up, another voice, a more vigorous voice, told me to keep going.

Every time I looked at that goddamn Boppy® pillow in my house, it would remind me that this could be done. This could happen. If Susan Matthews Brown could pop some stuffing in some horseshoe-shaped fabric, patent it, and call it a nursing pillow, then this SaraBear thing could happen for me. *She* did it. *She* made it happen. I know in my heart I could too.

And so it began. I would spend hours and hours researching what others had done, the baby-goods industry, and how to start a business.

One of the things I learned those first few years was a really important lesson but one that cost me a lot of time and energy. A simple lesson that is easier expressed than embraced: you don't have to reinvent the wheel.

That was what I was doing. Starting from scratch. Trying to figure out how to do what had already been done. A brilliant mathematician, Isaac Newton, when talking about his discovery of gravity and calculus said, "If I have seen farther, it is by standing on the shoulders of giants."

What was good enough for the discoverer of gravity should have been good enough for me. "Melissa," I said to myself, "get out of the hole you're in and get up on the shoulders of those who have come before you."

The wheel had already been invented, that is, the process of branding a product and getting it to market. But I'd been blind to the wheelmakers of the world. I was inexperienced and naïve and just plain ignorant as to how to start a business or build a brand. There were lots of good reasons for this. I was a small-town girl with basic dreams and education. I didn't have any business or real-world exposure. The farthest my sister and I had ever traveled as children was going to Grandmom's house in Pennsylvania in the summer. We played kickball in the streets and spin-the-bottle with the neighborhood kids in our parents' garage. We were raised very sheltered from the world, as many children by of the '70s were. We climbed trees, built forts, swam in the creek, and got stung by bees. We rode snowmobiles and watched *Laverne & Shirley* just after *Happy Days* Thursdays at 8:00.

All of this childhood bliss minus any cultural exposure or perspective, however, as it turns out, rendered me unprepared to do anything beyond middle-class aspirations.

So, yes. I was frustrated and annoyed. But I was hardly alone. Many women entrepreneurs who have branded and invented products started much the same way (for example, Noodle & Boo®, Patemm Pad®, BabyLegs®, Taggies®, and Boppy®). Moms who'd had enough, who had come up with an idea, who had to do *something*, who had to go against the grain of our lives to get to that point.

We all started our businesses in our homes, at kitchen tables, and the backs of our cars, and we just kept going with perseverance and determination, no matter what the setback or obstacle. In fact, those setbacks and obstacles tended to make us more determined and focused.

My problem was that I was chasing my tail. I didn't have the content to put into a business plan, because I didn't know what the hell I was doing! Sometimes still to this day, I take out my first "business plan" and laugh as I look through it. It is incredible to me what *wasn't* in it. No hint of P&L, net gain, margins, logistics, supply chain, ocean import, employee tax burden, warehousing, or cash flow.

The most incredible part of the plan was that I had spent hundreds and hundreds of hours on it, perfecting it. I viewed it in an almost magical way, like if I wrote it down really well, then my dreams would come true.

Not so much.

Of course, starting a business is not just a hypothetical enterprise. There is real time, real products, and real money involved. I wish my biggest problem had been writing the business plan. But there were more serious problems on the horizon than the miniscule—and turns out, unimportant—task of writing a business plan. I was using my personal credit cards and my savings to finance things.

To keep supply going, and unbeknownst to Benny, I had sold my last retirement account that held my last "liquid" cash. Ten fucking grand.

I thought I was staying afloat. But someone who knew what she was doing would have been able to assess my situation much better in a glance—I was sinking. Slowly but steadily.

My ankles were in quicksand, and my head was in the clouds.

And this was *just* the beginning of The Disaster.

Part II
Chapter 6
INSOMNIA IS A FORM OF TORTURE

July 2005...Nathaniel, arriving two weeks early and born via a you-better-speed-and-run-the-red-lights C-section, made his arrival and completed our family. Our very own baby boy. To this day, I do not remember a time in my life when I ever experienced such an overwhelming feeling of joy. During the four recovery days in the hospital, Ben and Sara would visit us, and we would just stare at Nathan with amazement.

There was a pleasant whirlwind around me, and for the two weeks following his birth, I experienced a bliss that even the Buddha would envy. I was bathed in contentment. My mother had seemingly beaten pancreatic cancer. She was her old self, or her new self if you will. Every few weeks after her first year in remission, she would come and visit, spending as much time with Sara as she could. She shared in the joy of my second pregnancy without the distractions of her own treatments, illness, anxiety, and struggles. When preterm pregnancy put me on bed rest and pulled me out of work, she was there at my house, cleaning, shopping, cooking, and looking after Sara while Ben was at work.

It was like an elixir to see the joy in her face when she was with Sara. For those times, the circle of life seemed complete. Grandmother. Mother. Daughter. We did those "girl" things together that are so enjoyable. Before my pregnant body put the stop to "full speed ahead" and took me off my feet, we shopped. We went out for lunch. We played dress up. My personal demons seemed to be at bay. Things were "fine" with Ben and I. Whatever was dissatisfying in our lives was easily dismissed. Hey, no marriage is perfect. Holidays were magical. We were doing fine. No life is lived without some trouble. I thought we were OK. Besides, my focus and my joy were really derived from seeing the pleasure my mom got from Sara and from being a mom to my daughter.

During the afternoon that Nathan was born, my parents finally arrived. I recall vividly watching my mom walk into the room. She looked different. A haunting trail seemed to float in behind her. Like I could almost see it...Something wasn't right. She was thinner. A bit pale. Fragile. I had the weird sensation that she was almost transparent. A darkness came over my thoughts, but it didn't hold. Part of me *knew* she was sick again. But I'd just given birth. I was still getting pain medication and was intently focused on my new bundle, not to mention trying to get some sensation back in my bladder so I could just pee.

I was in another world of postpartum euphoria. So I blocked any ill thoughts I had about Mom's health. Must just be my imagination, I told myself.

Once back at home with Nathan, I felt like our family was now perfect. The four of us. Complete. There was symmetry to our life that burrowed deep in my soul.

Perfect.

Benny and I took to our new routine of feedings, sleep (or lack thereof), making sure Sara got plenty of attention, and loving the baby. It was hot, the middle of summer, and Nathan and I spent the first weeks at home in front of the fan, absorbed in each other's love. I kissed his face and neck a million times, whispering promises to love him forever. No matter what. He was born into a family of love and promises.

Life was as perfect as it is allowed to be in this world. And then, to the day, *almost to the hour*, of the two-week mark of his birth, Nathan's reflux and colic problems burst into our lives, without warning, without subtlety, without kindness.

Recipe for Disaster

My heart was set and my mind was fixed on nursing Nathan until he was a year old. After Sara's colic and what we went through to survive those horrible, horrible months, I knew, without a shadow of a doubt in my heart of hearts that when I gave birth to Nathan, there was no way, absolutely *no* way that life would ever bequeath us another colicky baby. Just not possible, in the world of odds and fairness. There was just no way we'd have to go through that again.

I would have sworn my life on it.

It was fifteen months before Sara slept well—about five months of the shrill, horrible cry of the colicky baby followed by chronic sinus problems. Benny and I became zombies. I think we slept even less than Sara did. How we made it through those nights of crying in 2002, I'll never know. We were numb. Terrified. Unable to see any semblance of light at the end of the tunnel of our misery. Some nights we'd take turns driving her around in the car at 1 a.m. until she fell asleep. Ah, blessed sleep…but no sooner than the car engine shut off, her eyes would pop open, and her screaming would begin again.

We did and tried everything in the world to get her to be comfortable and sleep: Mylicon drops, drives, stroller-rolling in the house, Bjorn facing forward, Bjorn facing backward, walking, top of the dryer, in front of the dryer, swing with music, swing with no music, swaying, rocking, feeding, not feeding.

For all the mothers and fathers in the world with colicky babies, I will deliver to you the only truth we discovered through our seemingly endless months of hell. The only thing that works in the end, and I mean the *only* thing, the only magic answer—is nothing at all. That's right. There's nothing you can do other than wait it out. Nothing other than time. Lots and lots of time.

We were so dogged during those months that we could hardly stand. It took all our energy to just *breathe*. All the other things in life—eating, working, laughing, sex—oh, those things sounded so quaint and distant to our ears.

They belonged to a different reality.

We didn't believe we'd ever be "normal" again.

So, when we were finally past that horrible time in our lives, you can bet that I was sure, absolutely sure, that I would never know the horror of *that* again. No benign or loving God would visit such terror upon us a second time. I had faith in that. And it took that faith, that certainty, to even consider having another child.

I believed with perfect faith that our experience with our second child would be different. My second child's delicate little digestive system *would* be different.

I was going to have a joyous, delightful, nurturing young motherhood. I would breastfeed my baby for a full year. All would be well. I would know the peace and serenity of a content baby, of swaddling the bundle and sweetly laying him down for a night's slumber. I could be the mother I had dreamed of being.

So there I was when Nathan was born. Armed and ready! I had the breast pump, the nursing bras, the healthy food, the water jug, and the baby manuals. Bring on my happy, content, easy baby! This is going to be *wonderful*. I was ready.

But then, I learned that the universe can be a cruel jokester; I discovered that the Big Guy is not beyond rubbing our noses in our high hopes once in a while. He likes a good laugh at our expense. And this time, the joke was on us.

Friday evening at ten o'clock, two tranquil weeks after Nathan was born, I put him over my shoulder to burp just after feeding him. Like every other time I had done during those two magical weeks. I was sprawled out in my usual position on the couch. We were ready for that last little gas bubble, and then he'd be down for a few hours of gentle sleep. Calm and content. I was already thinking of the bowl of ice cream I couldn't wait to scarf down. I stood up gently as not to rouse him from his post-feeding coma.

Then...

Nathan began to squirm and fuss a little, and he started to cry. And the cry got louder. And louder. At the first nanosecond of the higher-pitched sound, I knew...I *knew*...exactly what I was hearing and the horror it portended. And I froze to the marrow of my being. I recognized *that* cry in the deepest part of my being—*that exact cry*. It was the cry of a colicky baby. And every parent of a colicky baby knows it.

It isn't the cry of an "ouch," or a hungry baby, or a frightened child. It is no ordinary cry. It is shrill and jarring. It carries with it a nightmare of sleepless nights and unsettled days. It is a cry that knows no comfort. It is a different cry.

And it was *that* cry that Nathan cried that night, without warning. That cry hits a certain frequency, a note, a rattling in the vocal chords. I'd heard it too many times. I still heard it in the direst of my nightmares. I *knew* what it meant. It was the cry of a colicky baby. That first time, he cried for only about two minutes. Two minutes. It might as well have been two hours. Those two minutes were an eternity. One hundred and twenty seconds of frozen terror. It could have been one second. It could have been ten. It could have been an hour. It would have been enough.

Benny, who was finishing cleaning up in the kitchen came blasting around the corner to the living room, dish towel over his shoulder, and froze in his stance and stared at me with a look of zombie dread in his eyes.

"What the hell was that?"

It was a rhetorical question. I could see in the empty fear of his eyes that he knew what it was. It was the sound of terror returning to our house.

I started to shake. I tried to pretend it wasn't what I knew it to be. I shrugged. "I don't know, Benny. He must have had a bad dream. It was a cry. That's all. A cry." But I wasn't fooling Benny any more than I was fooling myself. It wasn't *a* cry. It was *that* cry. Although I still held Nathan close to me, there was a part of me that wanted to push him away, a part of me that wanted to run, to run as far and as fast as I could. An emptiness formed in the pit of my stomach.

I wasn't feeling anything that Benny wasn't feeling. I recognized my own dread in the expression on his face. Benny trembled, and I thought I saw his knees start to buckle. "I can't," he said, his voice both emptied of feeling and strangled with pain. "I can't fucking do this again, Melissa. No way!" His lips quivered. "I just can't."

With that, he whipped the dish towel off his shoulder and stormed out of the room. I wanted to cry out to him, to beg him to come back. But I didn't. I didn't have the strength. I was lost and alone. And, the truth was, I understood. Part of me knew that if Benny had been the one holding Nathan, I would have done the exact same thing.

Nathan began to cry some more. And some more and some more. And then some more. Ten seconds. Ten minutes. An hour. Two exhaustive hours later, my little baby finally had no more strength to cry. He stopped crying and fell asleep. And once asleep, he slept like a little angel, peacefully. My exhausted, beautiful cherub.

Shit.

Just like he had fallen asleep every other day of the previous two weeks since his birth. An angel. My angel. I looked at him with loving eyes, but now my loving eyes knew they were looking at something different. Nathan wasn't just an angel. He was an angel whose belly was possessed by the colicky devil. Our blissful, perfect family had changed. Everything had changed.

As blissful as the first two weeks had been, that is how horrible what followed became. With that one cry, my serene, happy, blessed life was turned upside down. I become something less than human, a zombie tumbling headfirst into severe, endless insomnia and a nasty case of postpartum depression with a side dish of psychosis to boot.

It became, to put it mildly, a dark time in the Bramlage house. Our center was not going to be able to hold. Our wonderful symmetry was blown apart. Did it have to be that way? I don't know. But we were dealt what we were dealt. And, as any parent of a colicky/reflux baby knows firsthand, the only remedy is time. Lots and lots of time.

And, as it turned out, we had been functioning on borrowed time to begin with.

A new baby is always a challenge. Sleep schedules are disrupted. Feeding patterns have no respect for your "normal" schedules. Every parent of a new baby is exhausted. After all, it's not natural to be up at 3 a.m. working on two hours of sleep.

Recipe for Disaster

In the best of times, I am not good without enough sleep. My first job out of nursing school in 1997 landed me on the night shift in the intensive care unit of a small hospital. Twelve very sick patients, five nurses, and lots of coffee. By 4 a.m., I was pretty near useless. The blood would be drained from my face, and every time I'd sit down to chart, my head would begin bobbing as I struggled to stay awake.

Me and "up at night" have never made an attractive couple. Weeks and weeks of nocturnal existence with Nathan did nothing to change that. Hardly. In fact, they had the opposite effect. I could feel myself being hollowed out bit by bit, emptied of any semblance of the Melissa I knew. My circadian rhythm was on the fritz.

I tried to be strong. I had said I was going to nurse him and, dammit, I was going to breastfeed this child! So, as I'd been determined to do, I was nursing him. But being colicky, digestion was now tortuous for him. Shortly after each feeding, he would begin with "the cry." When I wasn't feeling bad for myself, I felt terrible for him. He just couldn't get comfortable. Before long, the only place he was content was on someone's chest, being held upright. Bassinet—forget it. Crib—not for very long. Floor—nope. Wedged in the Boppy®—for a little while.

It was the chest. Upright.

So there we found ourselves, Ben and me, on the couch, feeding, burping, bouncing, consoling, changing diapers, and doing something that resembled sleeping with a pillow tucked behind our necks and mouths hanging open.

We ventured into a world of trying to comfort our baby. We tried eight different formulas, three different beds (one special-ordered from Australia), stopping nursing, starting nursing again, stopping pumping, starting pumping, vitamins, special herbs, Zantac, Mylicon, X-rays, doctor's visits, a visit to the Boob Nazi. Too many fights to count and too many tears to measure later, we were beaten and battered. After four weeks, I could not deal with anything at all. The tiniest problem knotted my stomach. If I had to make any kind of decision, I was immediately reduced to mush.

To say that I was overwhelmed was a cruel understatement. I was so far beyond overwhelmed that I don't know if there's a word for it. I was utterly exhausted. I felt papery thin and hollowed out. I looked at myself in the mirror, and I could hardly recognize the person looking back at me. Who was that person with the pasty skin? Who was that woman with the dark shadows under her eyes and the terror in her eyes?

Could it really be me?

I was sinking deeper and deeper into some pit where the person in the mirror not only didn't *look* a thing like me but *wasn't* me. Day by day, I was leaving Melissa behind. Finally, I came to a day when I couldn't take it anymore. It must have been mid-October. I was aware of the brilliant, color-changing beauty outside the window, but only in the most superficial, intellectual way. Like I was looking at a painting of a beautiful day in a museum. I was so distanced from actually *feeling* any of the beauty around me that it was frightening.

At four in the afternoon, I walked up the stairs to our bedroom like a zombie. I closed the door behind me. I did not close the door with any plan, or thought, or self-knowledge that I'd reached the end of my rope. I didn't even make it to the bed. I lay down on the shit-brown floor and curled myself into a fetal position and began to cry.

One could make the argument that the ability to cry was a good sign. It meant that there was still something human inside my hollowed-out soul, something still capable of feeling anguish and pain. Of course, I did not appreciate that then. All I knew was that I didn't believe I could go on. I couldn't do it by myself. I needed something, somebody. I was sobbing. Crying for help. Crying out in sounds I'd never heard myself make before. Somebody help us! Somebody save me! I'm so tired, God. So tired. It was exhaustion like I've never known. I could not lift my face from that too-old, too-dingy, too-horrible for words shag carpeting.

While lying there, I had a weird flash, remembering reading about Guantanamo Bay and the terrible things that were done to the prisoners there. One thing stood out when I'd read the article: that with all the different forms of "enhanced interrogation techniques," one of the most effective forms of torture is sleep deprivation.

I almost laughed out loud. No shit. I would have done anything, anything in the world that afternoon, to receive and accept six or even four hours of uninterrupted, deep, peaceful sleep.

Anything.

As I lay curled up on the carpet, I then had an experience I'd never had before. It was the weirdest, most unsettling thing. My mind left my body and started floating above my head. Like it wanted to fly out the window. And I said to myself, "Oh my God, this must be where the saying, 'I feel like I'm losing my mind' comes from." It was like it was too much for my body to continue supporting the dysfunction in my brain, like it wanted to eject it. It was my body saying to me, "What a fucking burden, just leave for a while and give me a break."

And it scared the shit out of me.

I bolted up. Grabbed the phone. Called the phone nurse at my pediatrician's office and started blathering.

"Joyce! It's me. Melissa. I need help! I'm so alone! No one understands how tired I am. Help me. Please."

Her voice was soothing, but it grated on me. She consoled me; she listened. She was really very sweet but offered little in the way of real help. I was by myself.

"It'll be OK, honey."

"Thanks, I know. OK, take care," I said.

I hung up the phone, disheartened and reluctantly realizing this was a fight I was going to have to fight alone.

A few hours later, numb and dazed, eyes swollen and red, and feeling like I had just come back from a time capsule, I made my way downstairs to see how Ben was making out with Nathan and Sara. He was making dinner.

The house, it smelled like meatloaf.

Chapter 7

FINAL SCORE: CANCER 2, MOM 1

Life in the house approximated a very bad horror movie, a gothic tale in which dark shadows are cast from all corners and strange noises and disconcerting events happen. We were mere characters, caught in an ugly script. Was the house possessed? Were we cursed? Were we being sucked up into a vortex of evil?

Whatever was going on in our home and in our family, one thing was certain: I was losing it. Big time.

One morning a few weeks after my little brain-ejecting meltdown, I set out to take care of a simple errand. My cell phone wasn't working right. I forget exactly how. Maybe the battery just wasn't holding a charge. Whatever. It was a perfectly fine morning, and I decided I would head over to the Verizon store and get it taken care of. I won't say that I had dealt with my cell not working perfectly in the best way, but I wasn't dealing with *anything* in the best way then. Benny had finally managed to convince me that it was "just a cell phone" and not part of an extensive conspiracy to make my life more of a misery than it already was.

"I'm kidding about the conspiracy," he'd said gently.

"Well, I'm not," I'd retorted with a scowl.

Even on an easy morning, anything involving two small children is a major undertaking. Getting them out of the house—along with all the stuff that has to go along with them, from diapers to favorite dolls to sippy cups—and into car seats, all relatively quietly, takes a lot more energy than I was able to marshal just then. And the thought of having them both in the store…I was ready to give up before I even got started, but I had to deal with the cell phone. I'd been putting it off long enough.

As I pulled into the parking lot, I glanced at the time. 10:05. "Perfect," I thought to myself. There were only a couple of cars in the lot, and I pulled into a spot right in front of the store's door…where I could clearly see the red sign "CLOSED" hanging prominently.

"What the fuck!"

I pounded the steering wheel of my SUV. "What the fuck!"

"Mommy, don't say that," Sara said.

"Be quiet!" I snapped before pounding the wheel again. "Dammit!" I felt myself spiraling. I bolted from the car, not even bothering to turn it off. As the engine ran and the voice of the DJ spilled into the parking lot from the open door, I stormed to the store's front door. The store's opening time was posted right on the door: 10:00. I looked at my watch: 10:06 I pulled on the door. Locked. I peered into the store, but I couldn't see anyone. I hit the glass with my hand. Still no one. "Shit, shit, shit."

I went back to the car and got behind the wheel. I didn't know what I was going to do. How could the store *not* be open? They said they were open at 10:00. I'd done everything right, goddammit. Everything. I'd gotten the kids bundled up and in the car. I'd driven safely to the store, even singing along the way. I'd felt *good*. And now *this*! Why did everything have to go wrong?

"Why me? Why me? Why me?" I started screaming, banging my hand on the steering column again. I could feel tears burning my eyes and then running down my cheeks. I raised my head and stared at that red "CLOSED" sign, wanting to will it to flip over to "OPEN."

"Bastards!"

Sara and Nathan were frozen in their car seats, petrified by seeing their mother have a complete nuclear meltdown before their young, innocent eyes. Even though I could hear the DJ's voice on the radio, the hum of the engine, Sara starting to hyperventilate and Nathan beginning to whimper, even though I could hear the sound of the heel of my hand hitting the steering column, everything seemed silent in the car. It *felt* silent.

"Maybe this is what it feels like to really, truly, utterly, and finally lose it," I thought, experiencing a bit of the same out-of-body experience I'd had on the carpet only a couple of days earlier.

A couple of days earlier? Maybe it was yesterday. Or a year ago. Maybe I was *still* having it, and this was just part of *that*.

Oh my God, oh my God, oh my God, oh my God…I was losing it this time. I couldn't let myself lose it. Not now. I was in my car, in a parking lot, with my babies!

Then Nathan started to scream. As much as I hated that scream, it drew me back, if only a little. It centered me on *this reality*. I looked into the rearview mirror. Nathan was crying. Sara was looking out the window, refusing to look at me. She was pretending to be someplace else. Avoidance is a form of coping.

She had her mom to thank for that trick.

"Oh God," I whimpered. "I need help."

I stopped and stared with empty eyes at the Toyota logo in the center of my steering wheel. When had I stopped banging the wheel and gripped it, hands at ten and two, with a grip so tight that my knuckles were turning white? It took all my focus and energy to peel my fingers from the steering wheel.

I knew I needed help, and I needed it quick. But I didn't know what to do. My God, I was going to lose it again, and I couldn't bear to do that in the car, with the kids. If I did, I was sure I'd lose my kids. It made no sense, but that's what I was worried about: losing the kids. The police coming and taking them.

And all this because the Verizon store was closed when it was scheduled to be open.

I pulled my cell from my purse. I scrolled through my address book, searching for someone, *anyone*, I could call. When I came to my OB-GYN's number, I hit "dial."

The receptionist had no sooner answered than I started yelling in the phone. As soon as she heard me and how I sounded, she transferred me to the phone nurse. I was determined to get help somehow, but I was aware and paranoid enough to know how I must have sounded as soon as she came on the phone.

"You can't tell anyone I called," I told her. "You can't tell them I'm losing it. I'm a nurse too. There are privacy laws. If you tell anyone about this...Please, you have to help me."

The phone nurse remained calm the entire phone call. She asked all the right questions in a way that pretty much defused my fears. She asked if I was alone with the children. She asked if they were all right.

"Of course they're all right." I turned and looked into the backseat. "Aren't you all right, Sara?"

Sara continued to look out the window, ignoring me.

"Tell me again what's going on," she prompted me.

"The damned store is closed," I said, telling her about getting the kids ready so I could be at the store and how it was supposed to be open at 10:00. Just then, I looked up and saw someone in the store come to the door. She calmly flipped the "CLOSED" sign to "OPEN."

I stared at the door for a few seconds as I continued to speak to the nurse. "I think it's OK now," I said finally. "Thanks."

Before I hung up, we made an appointment for the next day. "Just for a check."

I stared at the phone for a minute or so before closing it and putting it back in my purse. Then I glanced at the kids in the rearview mirror. "Let's go in the store," I said, trying to force my voice to sound in control and cheerful.

Don't ask me how I muddled through getting done in the Verizon store what I needed to get done. All I know is that I got my cell phone issued solved and made it home with the kids safely, but surely as the most terrible mother in the entire world.

I arrived at my appointment the next afternoon. The midwife treated me like I was a fragile piece of glass, in danger of breaking at any second.

"How have things been going, Melissa?" she asked.

I stared at her like Marge Simpson looks at Homer after he says something utterly stupid. "You're kidding, right?" I blinked at her.

"I haven't slept in like three months. Nathan's been colicky since summer…"

She smiled the condescending smile of someone who had enjoyed a *great* night's sleep the night before, a blissful sleep without a care in the world. She wrote out a prescription for Zoloft, patted me on the knee, and told me that she was sure that things would start to get better real soon. That's it. No ongoing support. No resources. Just "Here, dear, you take these pills, and check back with us in another three months."

Fucking pills!

I stared at the prescription in my hand. Part of me wanted to tear it up. Another part was desperate enough to hope the pills would work.

After a couple of weeks, it seemed that the happy pills had taken a bit of the edge off. I felt maybe 20 percent better. It wasn't a light at the end of the tunnel, but it was enough to make me think that maybe there would *be* light at the end of the tunnel…if we ever got close to the end of the tunnel.

A few weeks later, I was beginning to feel a little more like myself. My mind was slipping back into the shape that was my head. Decisions were a bit easier; my insides were a bit calmer. The paranoia had mostly disappeared. To be honest, I don't recall how sleep was. Were we sleeping a lot more?

My mom and dad were coming together for a short visit. I was determined to get it together enough so that they wouldn't see me fraying and recognize the war wounds that lay beneath the layer of my skin.

I started looking forward to the visit. It would be great to have extra hands for a couple of days. Sara would get some much-needed attention. I might even have a chance to nap for an hour or two! And I was desperate to see my mom and to know how she was doing. Our phone conversations had been kind of cryptic.

"How're you doing, Mom?"

"I'm feeling all right. Better and worse days."

Like *that* tells me anything.

So, I wanted to see with my own eyes how she was. Well, it didn't take long. As soon as my mom walked in the door, I knew things weren't good. She looked papery thin, like if you stared at her long enough, you'd be able to see right through her. Like if she lifted a plate, her wrists might just snap. She seemed to have shrunk, so that when she was sitting on my blue rocker with Nathan in her arms, it looked like Nathan had just swallowed her up, and you couldn't see her for him resting against her chest.

Sara seemed to sense that something was amiss. Instead of running up to her and jumping into her arms, like she would ordinarily do, she kind of studied her warily.

"Give me a kiss," my mom said, opening her arms to Sara.

Sara moved cautiously, looking awkward as my mom put her arms around her and gave her a kiss. I could see in that kiss my mom trying to make it last forever. I shivered.

"So," I said, trying to sound cheerful. "How are things going?"

Dad shrugged as he settled on the couch. Mom looked away.

"We have time to talk," she said.

As it turned out, not a lot of time.

Mom told me that her last appointment didn't go as well as they'd expected. "The doctor found a 'spot' on my lung," she said, looking down and kissing Nathan's head.

"Yes. Go on," I said, my heart sinking into my stomach. I had the foreshadowing that no amount of drugs would be able to dig me out of this pit.

She shrugged but then fell silent, leaving it to my dad to fill in the details.

"Hell, it wasn't so much a spot as a little shadow. They're not even sure that there's anything there at all."

"Did they tell you anything?" I asked, not being successful in keeping the quiver out of my voice. I looked down the blanket wrapped around my legs.

Mom shook her head. "Just that they need to figure out what it is." She swallowed. "And what they will do about it."

It sounded, from her voice, that she was convinced that there wouldn't be anything "to be done" about it.

Later that day, as I watched her holding Nathan in the blue glider chair, I couldn't stop telling myself, "This is the last time she will ever do that." Of course, everyone was wearing a brave face, so nothing was said. But I still remember watching them pull out of the driveway to leave for home. Dad was driving. Mom was in the passenger seat, her arm just out the window, waving.

She wasn't smiling.

As soon as they were out of sight, I went into the house and opened a beer.

In a pointless strategy that has been used by millions upon millions of others who have felt their lives slipping out of control, I had begun to drink more. When Nathan first became colicky, it was just half a beer to try and get some sleep. Half a beer became a whole beer, which became a couple of beers.

My dad's mom, Mabel, had been a nurse. I thought it was kind of cool that being a nurse "ran in the family." It wasn't until later that I learned that being a nurse wasn't the only thing that seemed to run in the family.

No one in the family knew how long she drank, or how hard. What we do know is she stopped trying to hide her drinking in her mid-late years.

When Mom was sick and then after, I never understood how Dad didn't become an alcoholic. It wouldn't have taken much. Clearly, it was in his genes, and his life got pretty dark. But he didn't turn that way. His way was working seventy-hour weeks and smoking two packs of Marlboros a day.

Dad's always been cantankerous, paranoid about the government, and a bit crusty, but my sister and I knew he'd always be there for us. He might have been moody and difficult, but when things got tough, he would be there in an instant, ready to do anything he could to help.

I wasn't there yet. At the time, I was balancing the fine art of combining pharmaceuticals with the self-medication of alcohol. It wasn't working particularly well, but I was too deep into it to change course.

Meanwhile, back at the farm, that "spot" turned out to be a cancerous tumor in my mother's lung. Surgery was scheduled for just after Thanksgiving. When they removed it and ran the initial pathology, the doctor found out that the cancer had originated in her pancreas. It was back.

Now, looking back, I can see that there was a lot to be grateful for. After all, I had feared that my mom would not ever get to see a grandchild; would not get to hold her grandbaby; would not get to be a link in that chain of life. Nathan was only four and a half months old when my mom died, but Sara was just shy of four years old and still has memories of her grandmom, memories that I believe exist in her heart and soul and not just because of photographs she's seen.

My mom was a big part of her first years, a bigger part than I could have ever hoped for that morning that we'd gone to my parents' house to tell them that I was pregnant only to get hit with the news that she had terminal cancer.

But I'd be lying if I said that I didn't want her to have more time. Another hour. Another day. Another week. Another year. There are parts of me that are convinced she could have had that; that she could have fought—and won—more time.

***

On paper, my mom's last days at the Dartmouth Hitchcock Medical Center were as good as modern medicine can ensure. She was operated on. Fed. Cleaned. Tested. Medicated. And, pronounced. All by the book.

From the time of Mom's original diagnosis, she faced a lot of obstacles. There is nothing nice about being treated for cancer, particularly an aggressive cancer like pancreatic. Radiation. Chemo. Major surgery. It takes a toll on your body. It destroys your insides. It takes a toll on your will and your perseverance. But Mom turned into a fighter like we had never imagined. Maybe I should have seen more of myself in her determination. Maybe I should have seen that there always lurked incredible energy and passion under the docile domesticity of a meatloaf. It just needs enough desperation to try to break through.

For Mom, it was disease and the powerful desire to be a grandmother.

I was inspired by her courage and her strength: Every time I saw her read a book to Sara or hold Nathan in her arms. Every time I saw her eyes light up when Sara asked her to sing her a nursery rhyme song, or watch a cartoon, or just hold her hand. Every time I saw her with her grandchildren, I saw a woman who was determined to fight and to win.

I often felt a catch in my throat when I saw her with them. I was torn every time. I saw before me the truth that I'd always understood—that having children was a fulfillment of a deep, ancient imperative. A continuation of the journey of life.

At the same time, every time I saw my mother with my kids, I knew that the part of me that was *truly and deeply me* was being pushed down into the conventional, into the everyday, into a place where incredible pressure would either produce a diamond or an explosion.

I didn't have much hope of being a diamond-producing kind of girl. But I could feel the seething pressures, the molten uncertainties boiling hotter and hotter.

I saw reflections of that fire in Mom's eyes when she held her grandchildren. Could I last it out that long? To suffer through a conventional life long enough to find my "reward" with my grandchildren? Was that what life was about?

Or was thinking that way just another way of trying to suppress the real Melissa?

With Dad by Mom's side, squeezing her hand, she'd been able to confront each treatment and each setback, determined to continue to be a grandmother to her grandkids. But when the surgeon told her that the spot on her lung had originated in her pancreas, the fire went out of her eyes.

Why did he tell her that? Why couldn't he tell her that they'd found a spot that they had to treat? Another setback. Another reason to overcome the odds. Nothing more, nothing less.

But in that seemingly offhand comment—"the tumor in your lung originated in your pancreas, Judy"—the surgeon drove a stake through Mom's resolve. When she heard that, she knew that there was no hope. That the cancer had begun to riddle her body.

"You asshole!" I wanted to shout at the surgeon. "What were you thinking?"

I didn't. The real Melissa wanted to. But the Melissa that existed in the world still could not yet bring herself to. I seethed while the spirit seeped from Mom's body.

For a long time, I blamed that surgeon as if he was responsible for what happened next. Rationally, I know that blaming him is unfair. I don't think any amount of hope was going to heal her that time.

"Four years is pretty good," I said absently to the room, knowing my sister could hear me.

She looked at me, her blood clearly boiling. "What are you saying? It's OK if she dies?" she snapped. I felt my stomach drop. I was wound so tight. So worried. So unnerved that the "D" word was spoken in the hospital. "I'm sorry," I said.

Amy looked at me with her eyes growing moist. "I know."

I also knew she was right. Four years was an incredible gift for someone diagnosed with pancreatic cancer. But I didn't look at it that way just then.

"I'm going outside for a smoke," my dad said, getting up from the chair.

Amy and I glanced at one another. "Yep," I said. "You want me to go with you?"

He shook his head. "No. You should stay here. I'll only be gone a bit."

After the surgery, when they came to talk to us, we were like zombies. Time had no meaning in hospital waiting rooms. We could have been waiting five minutes or five hours. Who knew whether it was day or night. We'd gone through a handful of "false alarms" where doctors had come out and we'd sat straight up, only to have those doctors seeking other families. But this time, the surgeon came out, and his expression did nothing to bolster my feelings.

"The surgery went fine," he said, "but I'm afraid the news is not good."

I could feel my heart drop to my stomach. My knees felt a bit wobbly. I wanted to form a question, but my mouth wouldn't work and no words came out. None of us said anything. The background noise in the waiting room—the other families, the overhead PA, the general hustle and bustle of the hospital—faded.

We were with her when she was wheeled out from the recovery room and into a regular hospital room. Still groggy, it took her a second for her to focus, but when she did, she held our eyes firmly, as if to ask, "How did it go?"

I smiled as bravely as I could. Amy patted her hand.

"Surgeon said that the surgery went well," Dad said. It was true, but it was only half the truth, and not the important half. Still, she was reassured by the news and smiled weakly.

"How you doing, Mom?" I asked.

She nodded. "OK. Tired."

"You can sleep."

She shook her head a bit. "No, there's time to sleep later." She wanted us to stay. So, the three of us remained for the rest of the day.

At this point, we were old hands at the hospital drill. We knew all the nooks and crannies where we could go to hide, to weep, or to just try and find a little room to feel "normal." I knew where all the outside benches were, which elevators were the quickest, and which bathrooms were the cleanest.

Knew the seemingly endless hours sitting in a hospital room. The mounted television. The smell.

The last time Mom was in the hospital, the stay was extended. The days became weeks. Recovering from the invasive surgery to remove most of her pancreas took time. This time, the stay would not be nearly so long.

Unlike the six-week stay in 2001, this one was merciless and brief. Not long after the surgery, her lungs failed. I was watching the monitors by her bed, and I could see that even with supplemental oxygen, her oxygen saturation levels were too low. She was short of breath just trying to say a sentence. That afternoon, the doctor came in and decided that her condition was getting worse, and they were going to transfer her to the ICU.

I wasn't surprised. With her diminished oxygen levels, her mental status deteriorated. We were watching her disappear before our very eyes.

"What's happening?" Dad asked.

"ARDS. Adult Respiratory Distress Syndrome," the nurse said, sounding both sympathetic and clinical at the same time.

ARDS. Fuck. I could feel my knees weaken. When was she going to catch a break? When was her nightmare going to be over? Bottom line, ARDS meant that she wasn't getting enough oxygen. Her lungs were failing.

"What's going on?" Dad asked, turning to me. "What does it mean?"

I couldn't hide the tears streaming down my face. "It's not good, Dad. She's having a lot of trouble breathing. They're going to have to put her on a respirator again."

He made a face. He wasn't a medical person, and he had learned way too much already about all the indignities a serious illness can visit upon a patient. It ate him up to see Mom suffer the way she was suffering. "Is there anything they can do?"

"They're trying," I said. "She's just not strong enough to breathe for herself." I amazed myself with each word I spoke. I knew what I was saying was correct. But each word was like ash in my mouth.

My dad has any number of flaws, as anybody does. But whatever his flaws, he was the deepest level of devoted to my mom during her illness. He stayed with her, sitting by her side while she lay in the hospital bed. He held her hand and patted her dry, cracked skin.

"It's OK, Jude," he whispered to her over and over. "I'm right here. It'll be OK." Over and over.

Like a young woman watching an old couple holding hands as they walked along a path in the woods, I saw only the comfort and love. I was ignorant to the many years of unhappiness and strife that worked to sand away the rough edges on both of them. I knew how suffocated my mom had often felt in her life. But now, seeing my dad there with her…Well, it seemed almost worth it.

Maybe if I could just hold out through the difficult times…

Maybe.

But that was only a small part of the emotional stew that I was struggling with. I was sad. I was angry. I felt the loss of my mother before it had actually happened. And I couldn't bear the kindness and devotion of my father.

I was drowning. I couldn't understand what was the matter with me.

"It'll be all right, Jude."

I glanced at my sister, and then I looked back at my dad. Then I hung my head and just started to cry.

That night I couldn't sleep. Ben snored softly, sleeping peacefully. I did not even toss and turn. There I lay, stiff as a board, staring at the ceiling. I expected the phone to ring at any second with terrible news about my mom.

While I lay there, expecting the worst, I thought about a lot of things. Most of my thoughts began with my mom but then would trail off in all sorts of directions. About my life, my kids, my hopes and dreams. I thought a lot about when I was a little girl, recalling my mother spending a majority of her time in the kitchen. How she cared for us, always soft-spoken and calm.

I tried to think about when I was really happy. When did that happiness escape me? And why? What fork in the road had I taken that changed things? Was it a decision I made? Was it just the "curse" of growing up?

All I knew was that I wanted to feel happy again. Content, like when I was a little girl. I wanted things to be all right.

In the morning, I joined a rested-looking Ben in the kitchen as he was making pancakes for Sara. He looked up and smiled sympathetically at me. "How'd you sleep?"

I shrugged. "All right, I guess."

He let out a little laugh. "Who're you kidding? You didn't sleep at all. Look at you."

I knew he meant it kindly. It was kind of sweet, how he was trying to be sympathetic. But I was exhausted, and my last emotional thread was about to snap. "What? I look like shit?" I snarled. "Is that what you're saying?"

His eyes widened, and he backed off a bit. "No, I was just trying to—"

"Mommy!" Sara said.

He glanced at the kids at the table. "Melissa. Really."

I turned to Sara. Nathan was dozing in and out of baby-sleep in his bouncy chair, hardly interested in what else was going on.

"I'm sorry, honey," I said to Sara. Then I looked at Ben. "I'm going to make the drive to the hospital to see how she's doing."

"Aren't you going to have something to eat?" he asked.

I don't know what infuriated me more about Ben, when he was rigid and demanding or when he was really trying to be helpful and considerate. Poor guy, he was damned if he did, damned if he didn't. At least I had the awareness of a freight train rumbling through my emotional self. He wouldn't know what hit him until after the fact.

"I'll get something later," I said, leaning over and kissing Nathan on the top of his head gently, as not stir him, and then turning toward Sara.

"Hospital food is terrible," he said. "Let me make you something."

I straightened up and glared at him. "I said, I'd get something at the hospital," I whispered, making it clear that my mind was made up.

Like I said, poor guy.

I sat down and picked up my mom's hand. As I smoothed my hand over hers, I could see that her fingernails were cracked. My eyes widened looking at them. Overnight, even her fingertips showed the extent that her sickness had taken over her body.

"Anything hurt, Mom?" I asked softly.

She shook her head. "How. Areh. Thuh. Kids?" she said, speaking in breathless, one-word sentences.

I glanced at the monitor. Even with an oxygen mask, her oxygen level was only 89 percent. This is shit, I thought to myself. Jesus Christ. Just shit.

Tears began to stream down my cheeks. They dripped off my jaw and hit her fingers. If I were living in a fairy tale, the moisture from my tears would have magically healed my mom. But this was not a fairy tale. It was her life.

This was the end of her life.

"I love you, Mom. You know that, right?"

She nodded.

I drew a deep breath. I held her hand tighter. Then I leaned even closer and whispered in her ear, "I love you so very much, Mom. You're the best mother I could ever have imagined. Thank you so much for everything, Mom." I laid my head on her hand and cried. Her grip got tighter for a moment, as if to say "I know, honey," then her hand rested gently in mine. And we cried.

It was time for shift change. Amy had come back with my dad, and the staff, knowing it was my mother's last hours, let her sneak her baby in. Nathan and my nephew, Cole, had been born about three weeks apart. The joy at having our boys close together was bittersweet for both of us, knowing that our mother would never get to see them grow up together.

Amy barely looked at me as she sat on the bed with her boy. Mom reached up and stroked his adorable face. Looking on at this scene was too much for my dad. He began to cry and had to leave.

"I'll see you later, OK, Mom? I love you, Mom. I love you so much," I told her, gently kissing the top of her forehead, the forceful whisper of oxygen in our ears.

I hurried from the room and the hospital. I couldn't handle my emotions. I couldn't handle any of it. I needed to get back to my kids. I wanted desperately to hold my children. They were the only things in the world that made me feel rooted. There were times when I hugged them when I wasn't just hugging them, I was clinging to them, as if they were strong, thick-trunked trees and I was being blown by a fierce wind. If I didn't hold on tight, Lord knows where I'd be blown.

There were times I'd look at Sara and shake my head in amazement. "You were born an old soul. So much like your grandmother," I would say to her.

I got into my car and looked back at the hospital as I pulled out onto the roadway. "See you soon, Mom. I love you," I whispered.

But somehow I knew I'd never see her again.

The motherly instinct was calling me home to my children. I needed to hold them.

That evening, I was standing numb at the stove, stirring pasta in boiling water. My brain couldn't wrap itself around fixing anything more elaborate for Sara's dinner. She didn't want cereal, which was my first suggestion. Lazily swirling the noodles, I dialed the hospital to check on my mom.

I was transferred to the nurse's station in the ICU. When the way-too-perky nurse answered, I said who I was and asked how my mom was doing.

"Oh, she's fine," the nurse said.

Fine? I thought to myself. Does this person know my mom's dying?

"Still having a little trouble breathing, though. She's still on the mask."

"What happens to her levels when you take the mask off?" I asked.

The nurse said that her saturation levels dropped into the middle to upper eighties when she wasn't on a facemask with 100 percent oxygen.

What the fuck! I'm an ICU nurse. I *know* what those numbers mean. It's bad. Really bad. How is this woman so bubbly?

"Would you like to speak with her?" the nurse asked.

I was a little taken aback by the offer. When I recovered, I said I would love to speak with her. I couldn't remember a time when I had put a patient with SATS in the eighties on the phone to talk to anyone.

"Just a sec," she said.

I looked at the pasta. It had already cooked about a minute too long. But Sara was just going to have to have mushy noodles.

"What?" a voice said.

"Your daughter's on the phone."

A weak voice came on the phone. "Helloh?"

"Hi, Mom!" I said, startled to hear her voice, even though I knew she was getting on the line.

"Hi, honey," she said.

Her voice was the thin, cracked whisper of a ninety-year-old.

"Hey Mom," I said, my own voice choked with emotion. "Are you OK? How's your breathing?"

"I'm…I'm still having ahh little trouble," she said. "And this mask… They make me wear the mask. I don't like it."

"I know, Mom. But you have to wear it. It's the only way to get enough oxygen now," I told her. I glanced down at the pot on the stove. I'd forgotten to even stir it. I turned off the light under the pan.

"It's. Un. Comfortable."

"I know it is, Mom. But it's just got to be there for now."

I could hear my mom struggling to catch her breath. I shut my eyes tight, listening to her struggle. Tears seeped through my eyelids and flowed down my cheeks. "I love you, Mom," I said, struggling to form the words through my emotion. "I love you so much, Mom."

"I…I love you…too. Honey."

I was about to say something…What? I don't know, but the nurse suddenly came back on the phone. After struggling to hear my mom's breathless whisper, I heard the nurse's voice loud and sharp.

"She's doing OK," she said. "But she should rest now."

I nodded, not speaking into the phone. Yes, she should rest.

"She needs to get stronger."

I kept nodding. She needed to get stronger. For what, though? "Thank you," I said to the nurse.

And just like that, we hung up the phone. As I took Sara's noodles to the sink and poured the pasta and water into the colander, I thought about my mom's voice. How whispery thin it was. How weak. How strained.

It was the last time I would ever hear my mother's voice.

The next day, on December 5, 2005, in the early morning hours, her lungs could finally do no more. And her heart stopped beating.

The nurses, catapulting into reflexive action, shocked her heart once before listening to my father's plea to let her go. So, rather than enduring the trauma and indignity of chest compressions, multiple shocks, and powerful drugs, Mom was allowed to go filled with the sedatives they'd given her floating through her bloodstream and left to die with only my father's touch as he stroked her hand and told her that it would be all right.

I don't know if he believed it then any more than he had any of the other times he'd told her it would be. But he told Amy and me later that he was glad she was finally out of pain.

She had died, the result of a weakening that could not be helped. Her lungs had nothing left to give. Her electrolytes were completely out of whack, and her heart was just too beaten to withstand the insults of her disease. Cancer had finally won.

The doctors and nurses left the room. One nurse turned off all the machines, making sure there were no more alarms. She considerately dimmed the harsh, fluorescent lights of the hospital room when she left, leaving Mom and Dad alone, together as they'd been for so many years.

Later that evening, I sat staring at the wall in the empty house. Benny had taken the kids out for a little while.

"You sure?" he'd asked before going out the door.

I nodded. "Yeah. I really just need to be alone. I can't wrap my head around it…"

I couldn't. My mom was gone. Really gone. I'd been so frightened of this moment for so long. It had crept in gradually, but I still wasn't prepared for it.

"OK," he said. "Be OK."

I knew how considerate he was being, but it didn't touch me. I'd been numb to his goodness for a long time already. Adding in my grief, well, there just wasn't any room. For anything.

There was a pain inside me that I couldn't get close enough to even understand. I held my head slumped in one hand. In the other, I held a glass of beer. I needed something, anything, to dull the pain. The unending tears just streamed in floods down my face. Sobbing, I cried out for my mother.

The beer was a start. Not much of one, but it would have to do for the moment. I had been depending on it more and more to take the edge off the way I'd been feeling at home. The stress of my mom being sick. My utter disgust with my own life. But I had been half-assed at best about drinking.

It was mostly beer. That was my "saving grace," the only thing that kept me from swirling down into the rabbit hole in the blink of an eye. Beer has alcohol, but you have to drink a good amount of it before you really get knocked for a loop. And "a lot of beer" is an awful lot for a girl my size.

Of course, I was only forestalling what was to come. With my mother's death a reality, I was about to get serious about my drinking. I would stick with beer for a while. But not long. I would soon discover a more powerful elixir, a more potent poison, or should I say remedy, to drown my pain.

Chapter 8

KEEP. THROW AWAY. GOODWILL.

"One more second," I said.

Ben nodded and turned to the funeral director. "Just give her another couple of minutes."

The man, as waxy and lugubrious as you might expect of someone who works in a funeral home, folded his hands together and nodded. "Of course. Of course."

Mom was wearing the blue dress Amy and I had picked out. Against her breast were perfectly arranged photographs of her grandchildren with messages of love. A handwritten note from Sara. A photo of her holding a flower to the world. A flower picked for Grandmom.

None of those things would know the cold earth. They would be cremated with her and mingle with the ashes that were once her body, becoming part of her forever.

Ashes of a life that would never be touched in this world again.

Looking at the people who trailed through the procession line was like a "who's who" of my life. I grew up in a small town and had lived in the same house, on the same street, for most of my life. Everyone in town knew my family, just like I knew everyone else's family. There weren't many secrets there, as anyone from a small town can tell you.

There is some comfort in that, but for me there was mostly a feeling of suffocation by the time I was old enough to see beyond my own backyard. Walking into my parents' house—*my* house—after closing the casket and seeing her face for the last time was something I can only describe as being "surreal." Everything, and I mean *everything*, was exactly where it always was, but each and every*thing* seemed somehow "off." Like the way a room looks when you have a fever. Walking into the living room was like walking into those rooms they have in some amusement parks, the ones that are distorted so that the floors aren't level.

"You OK?" Benny asked me so many times I almost wanted to beg him not to be so goddamned comforting.

No, I was not all right. And I didn't think I would ever be all right again.

The maroon drapes with perfect creases. The wallpapered hallway with family photos on the walls. The school pictures of Amy and me. The small, framed photographs on the piano—Mom with her grandchildren. Mom and Dad, smiling.

There were industrial folding chairs plopped in the living room, so people could sit and talk while they were drinking coffee or tea and eating stupid cakes or cookies or finger sandwiches.

And my mother was dead.

What the fuck are these people doing in my parents' house?

Personally, I was a mess. Not just emotionally. I was a mess *physically*. I was never a supermodel or anything, but I had pretty much let myself go to shit. My hair was cut too short for my face and was a particularly hideous shade of orange-blond, a color that you can be sure would never be found in nature. I had let myself gain weight. My clothes were frumpy.

I was a mess. I could have been a full-year study in any reasonably good college psychology class. It wouldn't have taken a particularly insightful student to figure out I was falling apart at the seams. The trick would have been how to keep it from happening.

I was now a girl without her mother and, as it happened, it was my mother that had somehow kept me together. And there was nothing that anyone could do about her being gone. I was now walking the earth with body and soul separate. The few places left where I had once been connected, I was now torn apart.

I liked to think I came from strong, sturdy stock. That I was born and raised to withstand just about anything that the world could throw my way. But the emotional hurricane of postpartum insomnia that I had been through during the past few years had torn me free from my moorings. Through life and death, the joy of a new baby, then another: a family complete. Then, experiencing the greatest loss of life I've ever known.

All the while, meanwhile, back at the other farm, I was still trying—and succeeding (whatever that meant at the time) to manage the daily orders I was getting from SaraBear online.

In between grief and sleeplessness, with my vision blurred by tears and exhaustion, I was still making diaper caddies at three in the morning. I won't say it was a healthy or smart routine, but it was a routine. And any routine is better than chaos.

Routine or no, it was, without question, a miserable winter.

In February, my dad announced he was ready to pack up Mom's things. I hadn't been to the house since the memorial, and it was really hard to drive there. Plus, everything was so bleak in early February. The trees are bare. There are no flowers.

The landscape was a perfect match for my soul.

Amy was already there when I got there. She greeted me with, "He's already packed up her toiletries and jewelry."

"Really? Why?"

She shrugged. "I don't know. I asked him, but he just said that it was something that he was going to do."

"Can we go through to see what he's keeping, giving away, and throwing out?"

She shook her head. "Nope. He said it's done. Don't say anything, OK? It'll just make him upset."

It was my turn to shrug. "Whatever," I said.

Dad had taken charge of the task, assigning us to sort just her clothes and shoes while he took care of everything else. "I can't go in her closet," he said. "Her smell is there."

I knew exactly what he meant. As soon as I opened her closet door, I could close my eyes and imagine she was right there. I pressed my face against a couple of her blouses and breathed in the lingering scent of her perfume, and I started to cry. No child could ever be prepared for the unnatural and usually monumental task of cleaning out her parent's belongings.

Amy put her hand on my shoulder. "We should focus," she said. She said it gently, making me think that she'd probably done the same thing when she first got there.

As powerful and difficult as sifting through her blouses, sweaters, and dresses was, it was her shoes that gave me a really hard time. Hanging there, perfectly organized, on the shoe rack on the back of her bedroom door, they spoke to something that was true and essential about my mom. Her boots were arranged perfectly along the floor of her closet. Orderly and organized, just like her life.

And completely the opposite of mine.

That was Mom, though, petite and perfect. Purse always matched the sweater, and earrings matched the purse. Never ostentatious, but always accessorized perfectly. Classy. No one seeing her walking down the street would think her life was anything but under control.

We did set up an orderly process for going through her things. Three piles:

1. Keep.
2. Throw away.
3. Goodwill.

Each pair of shoes was a story. Remember when she wore these to work? Remember she wore these the night I graduated? I held her bedroom slippers against my cheek. These were the slippers she wore each morning, the slippers that comforted her feet. I closed my eyes, and I could hear the sound of them shuffling on the kitchen floor.

I looked at all her shoes. It was just so pointless. All these shoes, just waiting for the next steps she would take in them, but there were no more steps to be taken. She would never walk in any of them again.

"What do you think she was thinking?" I asked absently.

"What?" Amy asked.

"When she walked out the door of her home for the last time. You know, going to the hospital for surgery. What do you think was going through her mind?"

"Oh God, Melissa. Don't think like that. It'll only make you more sad."

"I don't think anything could make me any sadder," I said. I just couldn't imagine what she must have been going through. The fear. Did she know that it would be the last time she would walk through the doorway? Did she think she'd never see her house, this bedroom, again?

I was living in a strange psychological space that was divided between the past—before my mom died—and the future. The present was a series of tasks that I was trying desperately to manage. I loved Sara and Nathan. But I couldn't help but realize that I wasn't really *there* for them. I was torn and lost in my sadness and grief. I was devoting what energy I had to SaraBear.

Benny? He was lost in the shuffle. He was a body that occupied the same house, the same life, as me. But I couldn't deal with him as a fully formed, human being with needs and wants. I sure didn't have any energy for his wants or needs.

And even if I did have the energy, I don't know that I would have cared or if it would have made any difference.

That was just where I was. I needed every ounce of energy I had just to make it through the day. I filled all the empty space, all the energy, all the need. Benny spent a lot of time with Sara. I was with Nathan a lot because he was so small, my little boy, my little shadow. I held onto him tightly. And we became inseparable.

Chapter 9

TIDY BOXES

There are points in life when it seems like, one day, you look up and think, "Where the hell did the time go?" Whole days, months, years have flown by with a ton of things happening but nothing really important changing.

That's how it was for me after Mom died. The next two and a half years seemed to fly by in the blink of an eye. If you asked me what I'd done during that time, I would have been able to list the things that had occupied my time—raising the kids, working very hard, trying to make SaraBear a success, engaged in the same dying, hurtful, and numbing dynamic with Benny—but I couldn't have told you what I *did*.

Thinking back, the closest I could come is to say that I had something of a blind ambition when it came to SaraBear. Like the early steps down a slippery slope, I began with a certain desperation, then a glimmer of what "could be," and then a near fanatical determination to make SaraBear work. It didn't matter that what I *didn't* know was so incredibly more than I did know. I was determined.

Motivated by an almost religious fanaticism and passionate belief in my idea, I was as close to ignorant about process as you can imagine. But I was *in it*.

I didn't know then what to expect. And I didn't know then that in that regard, I was like most other entrepreneurs—insane. But good insane; that is, if you believe that having an idea that you are convinced is a great idea and then doing everything you can to make that a reality is good.

Regardless, I think it would be a kind and diplomatic understatement to say that I was devoted to making SaraBear work during those months, not that my devotion to SaraBear blinded me to the fact that so much else in my life was in a tailspin. I had begun seeing a therapist to try and "work out" whatever it was that was eating at me.

"Getting your head on straight" was the way that Benny described it with a supportive smile. He hadn't pushed me to go into therapy. I'd gone more than voluntarily. I was hurting, and I knew it. He knew it too. He was just as blind to what was coming as I was.

He thought, like I hoped, that the "Humpty Dumpty" that was me could be patched up and put back together again. He wanted the girl he had married back. I don't know who I wanted back, but I didn't think it was her.

In that realization, I suffered a certain amount of guilt. Sure, I didn't like who I'd become, and I was working desperately to change myself. Most of that was wrapped up in SaraBear and focusing on the kids. A fair amount was dedicated to reaching the bottom of a glass. Better stated, I *hated* who I'd become. But there were parts of my life I loved, and I knew I couldn't have had them without being whoever I was—that is, without being the person I didn't like.

I was suffocating in my marriage. But that marriage had produced the two most remarkable children in the world to me. There were times that I wished I'd never gotten married. That I'd had had the courage to just take off and travel the world, meet new people.

But then, there would be no Sara and no Nathan. That thought was unimaginable to me. So, I struggled with an emotional "damned if you did, damned if you didn't."

By late spring, early summer of 2006, the long winter was finally a memory. I was going to my therapist regularly, and with her help, drinking less became a viable option. She told me what was going on inside had to do with my mom's death coupled with postpartum depression. Maybe. Lord knows both of those things were throwing me for a loop. Benny liked that that was what the problem seemed to be. It kept what was wrong just outside of a critical zone where it had something to do with *him*. I enjoyed my therapy sessions in the same way I used to like the Lamaze classes Benny and I went to before Sara was born. Just practical enough and just touchy-feely enough to be kind of interesting and kind of helpful.

"So, why do you think you're having so much trouble dealing with your mother's death?" the sensible therapist asked.

I stared at her like she'd grown two heads. Wasn't that supposed to be what *she* was telling me? I came to *her* to figure that shit out.

"I don't know," I mumbled.

Way to be insightful and articulate, Melissa.

She pointed out that the loss of a parent is always a devastating event, but that in the "normal" course of things—she was quick to point out that "normal" is a very wide range—people begin to let go of their grief.

"And," she observed quietly and remarkably nonjudgmentally, "most people manage to deal with their grief without resorting to the abuse of alcohol."

I snapped to attention. "I'm not abusing alcohol," I insisted.

She arched her eyebrows. How did she manage to do that so that her expression was both pointed and unthreatening? There was no use trying to be coy. After all, one of the main reasons that I'd come to her was because I knew I was having a problem.

Of course, at that point in my life, being happy seemed as improbable as winning the lottery and buying a Mediterranean island. I was satisfied to settle for not-in-pain. Numbness was my goal.

Trouble was, I was falling short of even that goal, a goal that I felt was modest in the extreme.

"I just don't want to feel like this anymore," I said morosely.

"Feel like what?" she asked.

"Lost," I replied. "Vacant. Like I'm on the outside looking in."

She nodded her head. "I know," she said in that kindly way she had. "But it's going to take a bit of work to get better." She paused. "But I know that you will get better."

I felt a moment of real hopefulness when she said that. It brushed past me like a wisp of fresh air in a stuffy closet.

"It's just everything at once," I tried to explain to her. "My mom. Nathan being colicky. Running this godforsaken wannabe business. Stuff with Benny—"

She leaned forward. "Why don't you tell me a bit about the 'stuff' with Benny?" she asked.

Got a year? I didn't know where to start. I was talking about my mom and dad and then, all of a sudden, I was going on and on about the shag rug in the bedroom of our house. I was telling her about recipes and meatloaf and what a decent guy Benny was, so why couldn't I love him?

And so it went, week after week. The Zoloft helped. By "helped," I mean it helped me feel less hopeless. The pain was muffled. But so was everything else. The colors of life were a bit less drab. I was grateful for the relief from the emotional pain, but I felt like there was cotton in my ears.

All I wanted to do was to wrap up the whole "loss of my mother" issue and put it in a box and file it away. I had things to do. I had small kids. I had a business. I had a husband, for Christ's sake. I just didn't have any more time for this spiraling-out-of-control stuff.

So, week after week, I found time to go to my therapy sessions and try and feather out why I had such a fondness for beer and the bottle even when I was a young girl.

"So alcohol was always your source of comfort when you were feeling emotional pain?" she asked.

I was kind of dumbfounded by the question. I mean, I thought I'd always had a beer or two to have a good time. Wasn't that what kids did? Why did it have to be a problem? I just remembered being a kid. Nothing special. Nothing about too much alcohol. Just being a kid: Sneaking a beer. Sneaking a smoke. Going to parties. Driving too fast in cars.

It's what kids do.

It's just that, in my case, my therapist seemed to draw a straight line between something bad or upsetting happening in my young life and my drinking. This light bulb, this realization, somehow gave me some strength. And before long, I gradually lost interest in drinking. The allure and potency simply faded away. And I found some relief.

Recipe for Disaster

It was time to get on with life. My therapist might have sounded the warning, saying nothing had really changed in my life. That the things that were making me feel better now were really very superficial, and we were simply at the beginning of getting to the root problem. But I had shit to do. I was finally done with all the emotional management that took up too much of my time.

I had "dealt" with my issues. Tidied them up. I figured that feeling better was feeling better, and I was more than happy to take whatever I could get. Benny was glad for me to be out of therapy too. He was supportive because he had been unsettled by my behavior. But the truth is, neither of us came from homes or worlds that were so supportive of therapy. Life was what it was. You dealt with it.

I immediately went back to the process of compartmentalizing my feelings and my life. I set about boxing up my feelings in the same way I might box and pack furniture and dishes for moving. The more fragile things, I wrapped in an emotional bubble wrap and then placed them gently into a cardboard carton. But the end result was the same—get them in a box, tape the box shut, and send it away.

What I didn't really appreciate then was that feelings and emotions don't allow themselves to be packed away so neatly. No matter how much bubble wrap you have, or how securely you tape the box shut, they get out.

Always. Somehow. Some way.

But, for the short term, my demons were at bay. Some of them, anyway. Even when I was able to compartmentalize a lot, I could never quite pack away my feeling of guilt. I was completely and slavishly focused on SaraBear. Every entrepreneur will tell you that no start-up ever gets going with that kind of sick devotion. But what they don't tell you is that you *feel* the lack of everything else that you *should* be doing. Maybe Edison could sit in his little workshop and find complete fulfillment in his ideas and inventions, but I couldn't.

Deep inside, I was riddled with guilt. The entire time I was devoted to SaraBear, I felt guilt about fucking *everything*. Money. Time. The kids. My I'll-do-anything-to-avoid-having-sex-with-my-husband behavior.

I had demons that were stronger than guilt, but not by much. And to keep them at bay, I devoted all my waking (and a good deal of my nonwaking) energy to SaraBear. Through my mom's death and my mini crack-up, when my world seemed completely topsy-turvy, somehow, someway, the business continued to survive. Barely. But it kept moving forward. In fact, things were beginning to ramp up.

There were bright days ahead. I could feel it. If I could just hide from the ugly monster called guilt.

Then. One random summer day in 2006 when I returned from the beach with the kids, there was a blinking light on the answering machine. "Hi, this is Jessica with *O, The Oprah Magazine*, and I'm calling about your product for consideration for 'The O List'...words...words...words..."

Oh. My. God. *The Oprah Magazine*?! She had called looking for information about the caddy. The girl, who sounded fourteen, asked for a "press kit." My heart was in my throat. It didn't matter to me that I had no idea what a press kit was. It was *Oprah Magazine*! To whichever intern was calling me, it was just another call in probably a hundred she had to make that day. For me, it was like a ray of light shining down right from heaven.

After I got off the phone—and stopped jumping around and hooting and screaming—I went on the Internet to figure out what a press kit was. Nervous and brash, I figured I could put one of those together. So I cobbled together a WordPerfect document that seemed to cover all the bases, and I mailed it off.

God, I practically wanted to grab the postal worker by the shirt and shout at him, "Do you see where this is going? It's going to Oprah!" (Like she had any idea!) I prayed that my press kit was not one of the .00001 percent (or whatever percentage it is) of mail that gets lost.

My emotions and my behavior were a perfect example of what being a neophyte would-be entrepreneur is all about—some unequal balance between determination, naïveté, and inexperience. I was like a schoolgirl at my first school dance. Nervous. Excited. Thrilled.

Clueless.

Benny watched the business grow by small steps, helping with what needed help with but not being very aware of all the finances. Me…I just kept dumping money into SaraBear. I filed for the patent on the diaper caddy with yet *another* credit card—this one with even higher limits than the last one. Oh, and don't mention the new credit card to Benny. Or the last two before that. Or the business loan that Bank of America so kindly gave me.

All the money and credit was necessary to finance production and marketing. It didn't take me long to realize (after the Oprah intern never called me back), that if SaraBear was to grow and be successful, I could no longer have the caddies made in the United States. When it was clear that I couldn't do all the work myself and keep producing things that looked like I was working out of my friggin' garage or something (oh wait), it began to become clear that something had to change. At this point, I had outsourced the sewing for the cloth liners to sewers in the United States, and then I assembled them at my house and shipped them out.

The caddies were beautiful. The only problem was that it was costing a *huge* amount of money. In fact, I was *losing* money on product. I might not have a MBA, but I was pretty sure that a successful business was supposed to make money. Working with American sewers meant my margins were ridiculously low.

When I started out, it never occurred to me how important profit margin and volume were to running my business. My margins were slim, and I wasn't moving that many caddies. By the time the diaper caddy was done, I was making almost no money, and what money I was making was getting plowed back into the business.

"We've got to go international," I said to Benny.

He looked at me like I was speaking Chinese. Which, in a way, I was. I arranged to have a random manufacturer out of China make the baskets. Margins would be significantly better, I explained to Benny.

"But 'Made in China'?" he asked, not convinced.

"It's the only way this is going to work," I told him.

He shrugged. "I suppose," he said.

The baskets arrived to the house from China. Ben and I unpacked the shipment and then stacked and stored them in the garage. Our 32'× 26' two-car garage was filled with tidy boxes placed in tidy rows labeled "Made in China."

Over the next few months, I picked through the baskets to assemble and ship. As I did, I felt a growing, sinking feeling in my stomach. What we found over the next few months was something I could have never prepared for or dreamed of. Crooked handles, broken pieces, and warped wood, from sitting so long in a humid, dark garage. It appeared they had been packed in China too soon, before the wood was dry. As the hundreds and hundreds of baskets sat there over the weeks, my inventory was becoming destroyed, unbeknownst to me.

"Shit," I said to myself. There was no way I could send these out. Absolutely no way.

Ben and I saved what we could. We went through each and every one of two thousand baskets, packed in boxes of six. One by one, we saved the ones that could be salvaged and put the others in a pile. During the process, I had a batch of faux-leather replacement handles shipped over. In the evenings and on weekends, Benny and I used needle-nose pliers to take the old, warped handles off and replace them with the new handles.

One by one.

It was crazy. No way to run a business.

Benny sometimes made a remark about the Chinese workmanship, but I knew it was my own fault too. I hadn't provided any oversight. Lesson learned. Pricey. But learned.

When we were finished going through all the baskets, we dragged hundreds of unusable baskets to the mounded wood-burn pile at the edge of our woods.

"You want to do the honors?" Ben asked, holding up the gasoline.

I shook my head and waved him away. "No, you do it."

He shrugged and poured the gasoline over the pile of baskets. I wanted the pleasure of firing the fuckers up. When he was finished and stepped back, I took a match and threw it on the pile. Whoosh! In a second, the flame shot up into the darkening sky. Sparks flew up into the air and floated away.

Benny lowered his head, stepping back but ready to man the fire. Me, I put my hands on my hips and stared at the blazing bonfire. I stepped in a little too close for comfort. But I didn't care. The heat of it scorched my face. I watched the flames dancing, and it filled me with a kind of maniacal joy. There, in that bonfire, were thousands of dollars in wasted investment. *Thousands.* More than that, it was basket upon basket of "my babies."

I guess my therapist was right and my "issues" hadn't been resolved yet because, as the dusk settled and the flames rose into the sky, I walked, militarily, along the perimeter of the bonfire, laughing. My laughter rose over the crackle of flames, laughing louder and louder.

Part III
Chapter 10
HONEY, TARGET CALLED TODAY

There are times when, looking back, I think my experience is most helpful to would-be entrepreneurs as an example of everything *not* to do when starting a business. Instead of a businessperson, I was more like a walk-on on the set of *Crazy Housewives of Wherever*. I was unraveling, and the only way my imagination could fathom *re*-raveling again was developing my idea.

I know how it sounds. Who was I to unravel? I was a young woman with two beautiful, healthy children. A good, steady husband. Comfy house. Great neighborhood. I had it all. Except—I was like an hourglass with a hairline crack in it. The sand was seeping out, slowly but surely. The bigger problem was that it wasn't sand that was seeping out. It was *me*. Everything *sounded* just fine. But it wasn't. I adored my children, but I was losing my grip in being present with them. I was there, in the house, caring for them intently. But something was missing…a piece…a presence. I was always somewhere else in my mind.

I had lost interest in my marriage. The house was like a prison.

The only hope, the only glimmer of light, was SaraBear. But damn if it didn't seem that everything I actually did to make it a success was exactly the wrong thing to do.

Being new to the creative process, I was always too quick to let other voices get inside my head. When I first started SaraBear, I would make a couple of diaper caddies on my kitchen table and then take them to stores to try and sell them on consignment.

"These are real nice."

"What a great idea."

I just swelled up with pride when a shopkeeper would say something nice about the caddies. But I was very sensitive to every expression and gesture, reading them like a fortune-teller studies tea leaves. Did they *really* like the caddies? Why did they only ask for two or three instead of five or six?

One shopkeeper was scrutinizing a caddy when she said, almost to herself, "These would make really nice gift baskets." She handed me the basket. "Know what I mean?"

I half shrugged, half nodded.

"You know, fill them with baby things and sell them as gift baskets. Then the caddy is kind of an extra when you've used up all the stuff."

Jesus Fucking Christ. What is it with people? It's a product, a diaper caddy, a useful product for when you're walking around the house with a crying baby in one arm. The caddy can go room-to-room with you. The "gift basket" thing began to get on my nerves. I thought that was stupid. I knew what the caddies were for. But I was desperate to sell them, and I became game for anything so long as it sold my baskets. I was so anxious to do things right that I was like a schoolgirl, always anxious to please. No way my caddies were gift baskets. But, ignorantly, one can guess what happened next.

I tried to sell them as gift baskets.

Thousands of dollars of baby trinkets and toiletries in my family room later…I realized it was a mistake not to trust my instincts. It was a mistake to blur the strength of my product. And it cost me money. Lots of money. Eventually, you learn when you are trying to run your own business that everything costs more than you thought it would. And you will never make as much as you thought. There's a very hungry monster always hiding under the bottom line. And he eats profit margin for breakfast, lunch, and dinner.

God, when I look back at all the stupid things I did, I'm mortified.

I walked the streets of all the towns around where I lived, going into every store: pharmacies, gift stores, toy stores, consignment stores… You name it.

"Would you be interested in carrying my product? It's a diaper caddy. No, wait, it's a gift basket. Don't you know Oprah's intern wanted one!? Well, sorta."

The one thing I knew was that I had to sell the caddies. So I did whatever I could think of to sell them: Google Adwords. Three different websites and shopping carts. Pounding the pavement. Sending them to mommy bloggers. Cold-calling. Taking my own photographs in the garage. Naming them cute little names. Advertising. Sending them to *O: The Oprah Magazine* producers (ahem, three times). Expensive trade shows. Craft fairs. Giving them away to pregnant women on the streets (I'm not kidding). Cobbling together press kits and sending them to every baby magazine I could find.

I wasn't trying to be stubborn. I called all sorts of people in the industry to get some advice. "How on earth do I get to where I want to go?" I found people to be polite but tight-lipped about giving free advice in an extremely competitive industry. However, one thing became clear. Full product production had to move to China. Not just the basket, but the whole kit and caboodle had to be made in China.

After two expensive mistakes at finding the right manufacturer overseas, somehow, somewhere along the way, someone gave me a lead. And it was the right one! Before long, I had gorgeous diaper caddies and matching packaging in my hands. "Now. Now we're getting somewhere!" I thought.

Even with all my mistakes, SaraBear was growing. Slowly but surely—albeit maxing out on credit cards. Mortgaging and remortgaging the house. Taking family loans. Determined to make it work, I recruited my brother-in-law and sister-in-law to help me out at my first trade show. I had no idea how to work a trade show. I used wooden crates and pieces of scrap fabric as display pieces. Maybe buyers felt bad for us, but they showed interest. They really liked the product. One large buyer placed an order for a few thousand units!

I returned back home with some success under my belt, and, in an instant, SaraBear outgrew the computer table in our family room. I rented a studio office, hired a marketing assistant, and began down the path of fulfilling orders for boutiques and the large buyer while ramping up production in China.

Although I was navigating blindly like Mr. Magoo, somehow it came together. And so the dance began…Place a production order in China, import it via ocean containers to the United States, store the caddies in a fulfillment warehouse, fill purchase orders from stores, collect their money, pay the vendors. On and on and on, at each and every step teaching myself. Up at 3 a.m. to figure shit out and email with China. Eating a meal when I thought of it. Crying in frustration. Praying to God for help. Controlling excitement when orders came in online. Crying in frustration. Crying in frustration. Crying in frustration.

I was energized, excited, and very passionate about SaraBear. In other words, I was everything about SaraBear that I wasn't about my husband.

Things continued to look positive—not that I was making any money yet. Everything that came in went right back into the business. I was working as a nurse part-time and being a mom, mowing the lawn, making dinner, and feeding the dog. No glamour. But, it was clear by now, it wasn't glamour that I was looking for.

The first week of November 2007, I was standing where I often found myself, at the kitchen counter.

Ring, ring. It was my Blackberry.

"This is Melissa."

"Hi, Melissa. It's Celeste from Target Corporation."

Oh. My. Friggin'. Lord.

"Yes, hi, Celeste. How are you?"

"Great. Listen, I saw your product on a mommy blog that I subscribe to. I'd like you to come to Minneapolis and meet with us to apply for our Parent Inventor's program."

"OK. Sure. That's great! What's the Parent Inventor's program?"

"Well, what it means is that if we like your product, we'd ask you to ship us some to sell in some of our stores."

"Oh, wow. That sounds great, Celeste. Thank you. When would you like me there?" My brain was trying to grasp that I had actually done something right by sending free shit to the mommy bloggers.

"Well, I need you here next Thursday. Can you make it?"

"Absolutely."

"OK. I'll email you the details. And we look forward to meeting you."

"Sounds good. Me too. Thanks so much for calling."

Click.

OH MY GOD, OH MY GOD. TARGET CALLED! TARGET LIKES THE CADDY! THEY WANT TO MEET WITH ME! IN THEIR STORES! WAIT—OH NO. OH NO. OH JESUS…HOW AM I GOING TO GET TO MINNESOTA NEXT WEEK? BENNY IS WORKING. WHO WILL WATCH THE KIDS? OH MY GOD. SHIT. HOW ON EARTH AM I GOING TO DO THIS?

OK, Melissa. Calm down. You can make this work. Just talk it over with Benny. He'll have to say it's OK once he hears it's *Target*. This could be the answer we've been waiting for. Common sense tells you that if you're selling to Target, *of course* you're going to make money. Hell, you're only a couple of months away from owning your own island! Right?

Deep breath. Count to ten.

Ten minutes passed. My heart was still racing, but my reasoning mind had regained control of the memorable event that had just taken place. I was still standing at the stove making dinner when Ben got home from work.

"Hey."

"Hey. How was your day?"

"Oh, the usual shit storm. It was OK. You?"

"Oh, it was good. Just making dinner. The kids are in the other room playing." Pause.

"Oh. Benny."

"Yeah?"

"Umm. Target called today."

Three words that, as he was turning the corner of the kitchen into the living room, stopped him dead in his tracks.

Chapter 11

PETER V. PAUL

Entrepreneurs—even good ones—are solitary creatures. We operate in a bubble of idea and passion. Whether healthy paranoia or smart strategy, we hold things close to our chests. We try to be a one-person operation. But, after I was accepted into Target Parent's Inventor program, I knew I was gonna need some help.

As I mentioned previously, I had rented some office space downtown and hired some marketing help. In Andrea, I thought I'd found a perfect associate. She believed in the caddies almost as much as I did. I was fortunate because she was, like me, a young mother. She was also a very talented and creative copywriter. Her words jubilated off the keyboard.

They say that timing is everything. I don't know if that's true, but it's definitely important. Things were starting to look hopeful for SaraBear in early 2008. I was trying to keep my head down and stay focused. In my blissful ignorance, all I saw was the glass half full. Things were getting better and could only get better still. Which didn't mean that there weren't things that were very frustrating. Each day at the office brought an onslaught of annoying problems, crises, and operational issues.

But with Andrea's help, each day we navigated the roller-coaster ride of helping SaraBear make a solid footprint in the juvenile goods world.

Things started to pick up. Far beyond making the baskets on my kitchen table, full-scale production was now in China. SaraBear was shipping product to stores in Canada, the UK, and to distribution centers for seven hundred Target stores. In order to keep cash flow cyclical, I began factoring invoices, meaning I was borrowing money ahead of time, on the promise of a purchase order being received from Target.

I was as "balanced" as I could possibly be at that point. Everything seemed to be cooperating for the moment. My life was OK. My drinking was under control. Ben and I seemed to have an "understanding" that allowed us to seem OK. When we had friction, it was over how best to parent Nathan. I guess if it wasn't Nathan, it would have been something else. It was just Benny trying to be in control.

He couldn't very well tell me how to run SaraBear. That was completely my baby. But the kids…We shared them. So when it came to them, nothing I did was ever good enough. He would tell me how to be a good mother. How I should spend more time doing this, or talk to them about that.

Now, instead of just wanting to avoid intimacy, I began to feel a mild disgust. Disgust with me. Disgust with him. I didn't want to deal with our relationship, or lack thereof, at all. I just wanted to shut him out. I *had* to shut him out. It was the only coping mechanism I had at the time.

In fairness, while I was wrestling with all this, Benny was wrestling with his own demons. He hated his job at least as much as I hated being an everyday housewife. He was stuck. Stuck, stuck. But we needed the health benefits. We needed the steady income. And he was raised to be much too decent to make a break.

Status quo was the only tune he knew—even though it was killing him as much as it was killing me.

In April 2008, I took a leap of faith and took a hiatus from nursing, deciding to try and earn a full-time salary at SaraBear. But the stark reality was that I was borrowing Peter to pay Paul. With a payroll to meet and my attempts at advertising and public relations campaigns, I was spending a boatload of money, and there wasn't enough coming in.

If it wasn't for credit cards and the near-infinite kindness of the Bank of America, I'd have been dead in the water. They gave me money and credit. I spent the money and used the credit.

Within a few short months, I was up to my eyeballs in credit card transfers and money mismanagement. Cash flow absorbed every ounce of my energy outside of what was devoted to my children. I was determined to keep Benny in the dark about the real state of our financial affairs. Every night (and most of every day), I prayed to the "Tarjay" god to make me profitable…and soon.

I was working like a crazy woman, spending at least ten hours a day in the office, and that was only part of my workday. I was managing all the accounts and operations. There were hundreds of boutiques, plus Baby Depot, Target, and the distributors in the UK and Canada.

Even when I went to bed, I didn't sleep well. Dawn every day found me exchanging email with China, counting dollars, directing expenses, logging the factored invoices, deciphering Target and Baby Depot purchase orders, and directing the logistics of imports from Asia, and on and on…all by the seat of my pants.

And praying that Target would pay on time.

"Come on, Target. Don't let me down. Baby needs a new pair of shoes…"

By midsummer of 2008, the canary in the coal mine hinting at the coming financial crisis had come and gone. Orders were slowing down, and the calm before the storm was upon SaraBear. Being so wrapped up in the micro and with no options but to stay the course, in a million years, this small-town girl couldn't have seen what was coming.

I could feel the earth beneath my feet start to shift, but I was too—What? Focused? Determined? Stupid? Naïve? Desperate?—to do anything but bulldoze forward. Besides, there *was* really no choice. There was no going back. We were in it too deep.

Even though he knew as well as I did that it was a mistake, Benny signed a *third* mortgage on the house. But there was no choice.

"As soon as the Target checks start coming in, we'll be fine," I told him.

Andrea was an enthusiastic supporter. We needed the cash flow and she was right there next to me, working on Benny to convince him to sign.

I wish I could say that, despite being blind to the coming financial disaster, I was completely sane and rational. Ha! I wish. I was becoming unraveled. I was losing it from someplace deep inside me to the outside.

We are all held together by some deep glue—the deepest lessons and messages we learned as small children, the homes we grew up in, our experiences from watching our parents and other adults, our teachers, pastors...whomever. When you start pulling apart inside deep enough for *those* bonds to stop holding, you are really falling apart.

I was really falling apart.

I was constantly stressed. My expression was always strained. But, somehow, the CEO of SaraBear was holding it together in the eyes of the outside world. I was getting up at 3 a.m. to communicate with China. Then I would wake the kids at 6 a.m., make lunches, and get Nate to daycare and Sara on the bus for school. Meanwhile, I was avoiding my husband's touch.

I was the frigging American dream.

One day, triggered by a $25,000 unpaid invoice from an overseas distributor who'd gone MIA, I flipped out in the office in front of Benny and Andrea. *Flipped out.* It was a fucking major debacle. I was kicking baskets across the room and "fucking this" and "fucking that."

Up until then, oblivious to the fact that she was the only one actually receiving a real paycheck at SaraBear, my guess is that was the day that Andrea really saw the writing on the wall, and the message was pretty clear: trouble.

Sometimes I kick *myself* that I didn't see the financial storm forming. That I didn't scale back, rather than ramp up. But I'm pretty certain I was as oblivious as the rest of the world. How was I supposed to see it coming when so many so-called experts never saw it coming either?

My only choice was to keep going. Just keep going.

Recipe for Disaster

It was around August 2008, and the Ellen DeGeneres Show called. A producer said they wanted us to ship a few hundred diaper caddies to give away to their studio audience, a group of expecting women. I couldn't believe the exposure we would get. It would be fantastic! But then the catch…They wanted us to provide the caddies at no cost and ship them at our expense. I went back and forth for a while. The exposure could be priceless. But it was a lot of money, a big risk. Still, this could be the PR break we had been hoping for. I hemmed and hawed and contemplated and stewed.

"You should do it," Andrea said. "It's Ellen." ("Yeah, it's not your fuckin' money," I said under my breath from across the office.) Even Benny thought it would be worth the investment. That's what he called it—an investment.

My gut said no. So of course I said, "OK, let's do it!" We worked like maniacs to get hundreds of units shipped to their studio in time. Then, to our disappointment, at the last minute, they decided not to use them. They never even told us what happened to them. For all we knew, the hundreds of diaper caddies we shipped to California ended up in a dumpster.

Dear Oprah and Ellen, thank you for nothing and you can both kiss my ass!

I was edging closer and closer to the precipice. Anyone with half a brain and with eyes to see knew it. But I was losing it in the land of America, where reaching for the golden ring makes everyone crazy and losing your mind in the pursuit of riches in not simply "losing your mind." It is the price of doing business.

It's a dog-eat-dog world out there. Isn't there a lesson somewhere in the New Testament about not being able to serve Caesar *and* God? You can't do what I was doing without losing some of your soul at least.

Maybe.

I was about to find out.

But what they keep hush-hush in Sunday school is that sometimes you have to gamble with your soul to find yourself.

And that could entail nothing other than a trade show in Las Vegas.

Chapter 12
WHAT HAPPENS OVER VEGAS

Another trade show, nothing unusual. The Vegas show was the largest annual juvenile show in the United States, but other than that, it was nothing special. Just a lot of grinding work, no glamour. Long days of forced smiles and aching feet. Getting everything ready. Psyching up. Trying to make sure everything is taken care of before I left. I was so wrapped up in making sure everything was shipped that I didn't even give any thought to leaving until it was time to leave.

It might have been in Duluth for all I cared. It was just another trade show. Las Vegas had no real meaning to me. Trade shows are a grind. Unpack and set up. The days are long and exhausting. At their end, you collapse in your bed. Then you do it again. Pack it up. Go home.

Nothing about this trip clued me in to what might happen. What I couldn't have known was that the Melissa who boarded that plane was never to be seen again. She walked off a different woman. Over the years since, I've seen glimpses of that old Melissa, but the young woman who boarded the plane? Not her—she was lost for good.

As I headed to the airport, I tried to block SaraBear out of my mind for just a little while. I was thinking about my life. Benny and I had fallen into some kind of surreal relationship where we were both present and absent. We completely ignored each other even when we interacted with each other.

"How was your day, honey?"

"Good. OK, I guess. Yours?"

"Great."

"Love you."

"Love you too."

We watched cooking shows on TV together. Gardened together. Took the kids out to dinner. Smiled at the young waitress. Wondered what she thought—maybe that she would want a family as perfect as ours one day?

When we weren't talking about SaraBear, we would talk about the kids. What they had had for lunch, the milestones they were reaching. I masterfully shielded digs about how I wasn't doing things right with Nathan, and *that's* why he was fussy at dinnertime. We talked about our crazy schedules, which family we'd spend the holidays with. Of course, he talked a lot about his job, how much he hated it. I felt like I was doing a really shitty job of acting in a really bad "B" movie. There was lots of nodding my head and keeping my mouth glued shut.

We were a lot of things, Benny and me, but we weren't Hepburn and Tracy, or Bogart and Bacall. We mostly got along just fine. But that was because there were no rough edges anymore.

I sighed. Such a waste.

Before I left the house, I peeked in on both kids. They were sleeping so peacefully. Emotion tugged at my heart as I looked in on them snuggled in their beds. "God, I love you," I whispered into their rooms. I blew kisses in the air and carefully shut their doors. The dog picked up his head to see what the movement was about and then went right back to sleep. I tip-toed away from my bedroom door. *Shhhhhh...*

It was still dark when I snuck out of the driveway, not disturbing a soul.

By 6:30 a.m. I was sitting in the boarding area of Gate B at Albany International. Mostly oblivious to everyone and everything around me, I hammered away at my laptop, obsessively adjusting an operating expense or two in the SaraBear spreadsheets. It was like a game. Moving numbers. Analyzing where to cut back, where to increase sales. The minute details engulfed me, distracting me from the fundamental fear that this "caddy thing" just wasn't going to work.

In it too deep, I had no choice but to ignore the macro and focus on the micro. Typing and retyping numbers on a spreadsheet: I could do that. I had control over that.

Just like a game.

Stupid, stupid, naïve girl.

"Rows one through thirty may begin boarding..."

The voice over the loudspeaker filtered through my fog. I shut my computer and slipped it into my bag. I rubbed my face to get some blood moving and then stood up. In front of me, a man walked over to preboard.

"Red Sox fan," I thought as his Boston hat caught my eye.

I glanced down and saw he was wearing open-toe sandals. Interesting get up. I sighed.

That was it. Nothing more. Nothing less. If you asked me about anyone else in the boarding area that morning, anyone else on the plane, I couldn't have come up with a single face, feature, or characteristic. If you said that the future of the republic depended on my remembering whether or not a tall girl with red hair was seated in front of me, or an overweight gray-haired man had bumped me in line, or a college student with acne scars and a sparse beard had asked me to watch his bag, the republic would have been doomed.

I didn't notice anyone. But I noticed him.

Like herding animals, we moved forward onto the plane.

Wouldn't you know it? Mr. Red Sox was standing in the aisle of my row, putting his bag in the overhead compartment.

"Do you mind?" I asked, nodding in the direction of the window seat.

The trace of a smile crossed his face. "No. Not at *all*."

I didn't hear his voice so much with my ears. I heard it somewhere deep in my soul, and it caused a stirring that I didn't recognize. He had, without question, the sexiest voice I'd ever heard.

I don't know how long I stood there as he stepped aside. Probably no more than half a second. Then I brushed by him and sat down. As I let my head fall back, I had no way of knowing that the woman I had become had only a very few more moments to exist before she was gone forever.

He slipped into the aisle seat next to me. I glanced out the window. His reflection was there.

The plane took off and just like that, everything changed.

"Ever been to Vegas before?"

"I'm sorry?" I said, turning to face him but keeping my eyes down. I was a bit annoyed he was talking to me so early in the flight.

"Have you ever been to Vegas before?" he asked again.

I shook my head. "Yes, once. But…I'm just an upstate girl. Don't travel much." I barely smiled.

He looked over my way for a moment. "You don't look like just an upstate girl," he muttered softly.

I'm not, I'm not, I'm not, I'm not, I'm not, I'm not…

As the plane taxied, took off, and found its cruising altitude, he asked me question after question. Who was I? What did I do? No one had ever seemed so interested in *me* before. No one had ever cared enough to *ask* me what I did, why I did it, and how I felt about it.

So I told him. About SaraBear. About my dreams. As I did, I noticed that he wasn't just nice hair and leather sandals. His clothes were nice. Casual nice. His hands were clean, and his nails were manicured. Even his toes had been manicured. SaraBear was in financial dire straits, and I needed an investor, a fiscal miracle. Could this be the person who would save me from financial ruin?!

Who was this guy?

We're two hours into the flight and exchanging laptops, letting each other look at various works. I'm trying desperately to show him the value in what I'd created; he's not hearing what I'm saying. But we're laughing and teasing one another like we've been friends for a hundred years. But not exactly friends. I was experiencing something both familiar and strange.

He was flirting with me. Or was it I flirting with him? I hadn't felt that…*young* in a long, long time. By the time we were in the air space over the Grand Canyon, he was on his third vodka tonic. I was on my second Coke. For three hours we'd talked and laughed, but I had

Recipe for Disaster

avoided direct eye contact. I'd glanced sideways at him. Or looked at my laptop. Or my hands. Or his hands. But not his eyes. Not his eyes.

Then, he turned and looked directly at me.

Shit.

What was *that*? What was the feeling I was feeling?

At first our touches were light, friendly. Laughing. Goofing. We explored strengths and weaknesses. What lifetime ago had I first met him?

He was like Tom Sawyer, exaggerating. I was the schoolgirl, underplaying my accomplishments. I knew he was full of shit, but I laughed anyway. He knew exactly what I'd managed to accomplish.

For four and a half hours, my world was two seats in aisle five, Delta Airlines. Despite the frisson, I was relaxed. Comfortable. Content.

I felt alive.

Which was both delightful and confusing. It seemed so long since that Melissa had ventured into the world. And, while she was tentative at first, she was quickly coltish, then brave.

The more he talked, the more intrigued I became. I watched his fingertips move softly around the perimeter of his glass. I could not help but wonder about the feel of those fingertips. I watched him longer than I knew I should have. He knew it too.

"As we begin our descent into Las Vegas…"

What? Where did the flight go? It seemed to have gone by in the blink of an eye. "Oh my God, Melissa," I thought to myself. "Only you can be cruising at thirty-two thousand feet and get hit by a fucking freight train."

Mr. Boston (aka Matt) was talking, but I was only pretending to listen now. Attuned to me, he stops and looks at me. I try to look away, but he holds me in his gaze. I had noticed his eyes were beautiful, but it was only then that I saw how unbelievably dark and deep they were. Inviting. Seductive.

I tried to look away. He shifts his head, staying in my field of vision.

"You know, Melissa, you're very beautiful."

I felt butterflies in places I didn't even know I had places. My mouth opened, but no sound came out. My eyes widened. I could feel a prickly heat on my cheeks. Up until that moment, no man had ever told me I was beautiful. And *very* beautiful? I lowered my eyes, almost as if I was shamed by the compliment. My God, I was a married woman! My entire body uncomfortably flushed. Still, I was smiling just a bit.

Four words: you are very beautiful. Four words, and my life changed.

Before the plane touched down, Matt turned to me again. "Dinner? No commitment," he added quickly. "In the airport. I want to buy you dinner."

Dinner? I was shocked. Flustered. Appalled. Thrilled. I'm a married woman. I couldn't have dinner with a man I'd just met on an airplane. But then, it was *only* dinner. What was the big deal? No, I couldn't. I just couldn't. I am happily married! I tried to explain to Matt that I had really enjoyed meeting him, but dinner was out of the question. But almost nothing would come out of my mouth! Suddenly, I was very uncomfortable in my seat. Edgy. Fidgety. I wanted to get up. I wanted to run. I wanted to stay.

I wanted something, but I was not sure what it was.

What was I thinking? Was I out of my mind?

I turned and stared out the window, trying to fake interest in the artificial landscape of Sin City.

"Are you all right?" he asked.

I nodded, not turning to look at him. "Yes," I said, finding my voice again. "Just hungry, I guess. And I've had enough of sitting."

He smiled a smile that was, I imagined, exactly how the cat would smile when he knew the mouse was his. But it was sweet. And the truth was, he was way ahead of me. Something was stirring inside of me. Something had been woken; a hibernating monster had been disturbed. I could feel something invisible wrap around me, like a seeping gas from the city streets.

The sensation…It was vaguely familiar. What the hell was wrong with me? What the hell was this?

And Matt just smiled. I couldn't look him in the eyes. If I did, I knew I'd be in trouble. I couldn't talk either.

The plane finished taxiing to the gate. *Ding.* The hustle of passengers grabbing their bags and things began. People crowded the aisle, and I was forced to stand close to Matt, our hips touching. Whoa. My insides were like a volcano about to erupt. I quickly grabbed my carry-on.

"Take care," I said softly, keeping my eyes down. Then I started down the aisle. Eyes down. Focus. Focus. Focus. Don't think, Melissa. Just keep walking. Quickly.

I scuffled off the plane, beelining for baggage claim. Dammit, I could *feel* his eyes on me. He was devouring my backside silhouette with his eyes. I knew he was staring at my ass in my tight jeans. I knew it, and I *loved* it. But I couldn't look back. I couldn't.

With each step, the flight replayed in my mind. I didn't remember everything we said, just the sensations. The smell of vodka tonic on his breath. Which was delicious. His clothes. His eyes. His goddamned baseball cap. His damned eyes. They owned me! They told stories. They seduced.

I needed to stop and gather myself. Christ! I jettisoned through the airport, trying to get lost in the crowd. There was a bathroom up ahead; I ducked in. Just inside the doors, with a careless thump, I dropped my shoulder bags on the floor and paused. I then walked over to the counter. "Who the fuck *are* you?" I asked myself before splashing cold water on my face. I was breathing deeply. My heart was racing. I leaned forward, my arms spread out before me on the counter. Slowly I looked up at myself in the mirror. My cheeks were flushed. My hair was a tousled mess. There was something about the person I was looking at that was different. She was askew, eyes bright green, shirt wrinkled, totally maddened. The woman looking back at me was…sexy. For the first time, maybe in my whole life, I looked sexy.

And all of a sudden, everything I was feeling felt vaguely familiar. Visceral. I closed my eyes, but in the darkness behind my eyelids, all I saw were Matt's brown eyes. His deep, dark, seductive eyes.

And then it hit me like that freight train. The feeling I was experiencing…

It was *desire*. Incredible, insatiable desire. And it had been a lifetime since I had felt it.

Matt had written something on a business card somewhere over the heartland of America. I quickly rummaged through my bag. Found it. There it was.

I had his name and number.

And with those two things, an upstate girl's journey to the bottom began.

Chapter 13

PACING THE FLOOR

Call me stupid. Lord knows, I've called myself stupid about this enough times. There had been a time when I thought of myself as smart—not brilliant or anything, but smart enough. And not just school smart: smart enough to stay out of trouble. Smart enough to put together a decent life, even if that life was a tad uninspired.

I worked my butt off. I was focused on the success of the trade show and SaraBear. But in all my laser-like focus on my product, I kind of missed out on a significant piece of information—the whole world was in the middle of the largest economic implosion since the Great Depression. The proverbial shit wasn't *about* to hit the fan; it was already happening, and its collateral damage was going to be enormous.

This tsunami of an economic shit storm would have an immediate effect on me and my life. Sales of consumer goods were slowing to a trickle. Moving a juvenile-goods product was like swimming in quicksand.

Sales were in the toilet at the trade show. The big buyers were nowhere to be found. Even individual buyers were few and far between. Any illusion I had that this trade show would be like the year before, when sales had seemed to make themselves, was about to be slammed.

My trading floor mantra became, "What the fuck? What the fuck?" I paced back and forth, shaking my head, these words slipping through my dry lips. "What the fuck?"

The year before, the display floor had been packed. Now, it was sparse.

By the afternoon of the second day, I was really starting to lose it. Andrea was reduced to nothing other than keeping me distracted and happy, neither of which I wanted to be paying for her to do! My whole life was dead on the line and having her asking me if I wanted another bottle of water was more than I could take.

"No, I do not want any more fucking water!" I snapped.

"Come on, Melissa. It'll get better," she gamely argued.

I looked at her like she was a foreign intruder. "Really? Look around you. You see anyone here who's going to buy our stuff? No? Me either!"

I was thinking of her as a total waste of time and money. Unfair, true. Looking back, it wasn't like there was anything she *could* have done. We were all being carried along by realities that we couldn't control.

My "friends" in the industry—colleagues and fellow entrepreneurs who had been sounding boards and someone to have a drink with after a long day on the convention floor—were all making themselves scarce. With so few buyers, we were all living the law of the jungle, each one of us out for his or her own interests. The "pie" had shrunk to the size of a Pop-Tart. There wasn't enough for each of us to get a piece.

The first time Matt called, I felt a jolt of excitement. But I couldn't keep my frustration from our conversation. "You cannot imagine how this all sucks," I told him.

He laughed and said he was sure it would get better.

"Yeah, sure," I said.

He called again, late in the afternoon on the second day. If anything, the situation on the display floor had gotten worse. "I thought you said things would get better," I said to him, unable to keep a flirty tone out of my voice. Andrea looked over at me with a curious look, like "Who the hell are you talking to?"

"I promise. What do you say I help you out?"

"Really? And how exactly do you propose you are going to do that?"

He chuckled in one of those "that's for me to know and you to find out" kind of ways. Then he said softly, "I have some money to invest. Maybe we could make this work for both of us."

My heart quickened, as if it wasn't beating hard enough just talking to him. I kept telling myself to calm down. Damn, I felt like I was in junior high school again. But it was a pretty heady mix—flirting and money. The man was offering me the two things I desperately needed.

And wanted.

"So here's what I propose," he said in a soft voice that was hard for me to hear. "It's really a win-win for you."

"I'll be the judge of that," I teased.

He chuckled again.

"So?" I eased myself away from Andrea so I could talk. "What's the proposition?"

It turned out to be a very straightforward proposition. And one as old as history itself. He had money to invest, and he was glad to invest it. On one condition.

I felt my stomach drop. Not that I wasn't *interested* in having sex with him. Hell, to paraphrase that line from *Jerry Maguire*, he practically had me at "hello." But this didn't have a lot of romance to it, not even with his sexy voice. It wasn't that I didn't *want to*. It was more that I didn't know *how to*. How do I reply to that offer? Sure, he had practically swept me off my feet in the plane, but I was still, when push came to shove, the same old Melissa. Naïve mother of two. Unhappily married, living in a small town.

Hell, I didn't *do* things like that. A weird, disembodied voice played through my brain: "I'm not that kind of girl."

I wasn't.

Nobody I knew was.

I looked around, like I was on some kind of perverse "Candid Camera" or something. I started to say something, but no words seemed to be able to make their way through my throat.

"Hey, you still there?"

I nodded, like *that* told him anything. Finally, I managed to squeak out a "Yes. I'm still here."

With that, he not only proceeded to lay on the charm, but he started to negotiate as well. "Come on, this is a great deal. I know you're interested. You were interested even before we were talking about investments."

Yeah, sure. He was right. So what? No one said that I hadn't let that fantasy play through my mind a whole lot of times up at thirty-six thousand feet. Hell, it was practically on a continual loop. But that was harmless. This was…This was something *real.* Way too real for someone like me.

"Hey, that's real flattering," I said, using the only trick that I had, the one that girls all learn at an early age because the world is filled with predators—I tried to buy time. "And I'm not going to lie. It's a compelling offer…" (That's right, Melissa, keep it honest *and* light. Have an exit strategy. Exit strategy…Hell, I didn't have an exit strategy!) "But I'm completely unnerved here. Business has me all in a funk. Can we just kinda keep this about business for a stretch?"

"But I *am* talking about business," he replied, with just enough of a lecherous tone to be doubly attractive.

"Very funny," I said, my light laugh sounding awfully strained to my own ears.

"I'm not being funny," he said, laughing himself.

"Listen, why don't we fly back to New York together," I said. "We can talk about…business."

I could practically *hear* him smiling on the other end of the line.

Why don't we fly back to New York together? What was I thinking?

The truth? I was thinking a lot of things, and feeling a whole lot more. That "carrot" of investment money was almost as seductive to me as his eyes. The combination of how he'd gotten under my skin and the possibility of his "rescuing" me from my financial situation was a heady mix.

"Sounds good," he said. "Talk to you later."

And there I was, standing in the middle of the floor of the Las Vegas convention center, holding my cell to my ear with no one on the line.

"Who the heck was that?" Andrea asked, looking at me funny.

God, could she *see* the turmoil in my belly? "No one," I stammered. "Hopefully someone who can invest in the business."

She narrowed her eyes at me. "An investor?" she asked suspiciously.

I snapped at her, telling her to tend to the booth. I needed to pee. As I marched myself toward the restrooms, I knew that my snapping at her and changing the subject had told her more than I wanted. I felt exposed.

I stood in the bathroom and splashed cool water on my face. Just like at the airport, I stared at my reflection in the mirror and asked myself, "Who *are* you?"

Only a couple of days earlier I could have answered that question. I might not have been thrilled with the answer, but I would have had one.

I didn't now.

Just then, the door opened, and an older woman with way too many convention centers under her belt came in. "It's brutal out there," she said, seeing me.

I nodded. "Never seen anything like it."

She shrugged. "I guess we shouldn't be surprised, not with how the stock market's tanking."

The stock market was tanking? My God, had I been living in a bubble?

Over the next couple of days, Matt's phone calls continued to get under my skin in prickly, uncomfortable/exhilarating ways. I was so far from my comfort zone that I was sure I'd never find my way back. But I *liked* it. I felt alive.

Every time he called, I tried to steer the conversation toward business, but he was an expert at staying vague, letting me know just enough to want more. As it turned out, he was a master of seduction, a spider so expert at weaving a web that the fly had no idea what was happening.

With each call, his voice, his tone, his words tugged at the bonds that had held me to *me*. I was coming unglued, and I felt more alive than I'd ever felt before in my life. He was peeling back layers of me that I hadn't known existed, exposing me to a rawness that made my nerves twitch. I wanted more and more and more.

***

By the third night, I hadn't had more than four or five hours of sleep in Las Vegas. The city's famed insomnia was kicking in and taking its toll. I was a zombie, yet exhilarated and alive at the same time.

I spent the long, endless days pacing the convention center floor in a numbing and frustrating exercise. I would emerge at the end of the day to a blast of "real" Las Vegas desert air—as if anything in Vegas is real. Even though I could get to my hotel room without going outside, I was determined to feel real air on me a little every day. I was determined to feel something *real* every day. I was losing my grip, and I had to believe that there was still a little something I could touch that made sense to who I was and who I'd always been. I'd rinse off in the shower and, unable to sleep, put on my light sundress and head to the pool.

As I sat with my feet in the blue water, I found myself texting with Matt. This was my first experience with texting, and my efforts to write complete, grammatically correct sentences were as comical as me trying to interpret the abbreviations he used effortlessly.

I must have been sending out some kind of new vibe, because there I was, lounging by the pool in a simple sundress, when a good-looking, young guy came and sat down next to me.

"You here alone? Get you something to drink?"

I smiled and took my earbuds from my ears, cutting off the Sting album. "I'm sorry?"

"How are you?" he said, enunciating each word clearly and punctuating them with a bright smile.

"I'm good, thanks." I was, too. I'd been listening to Sting and just letting myself drift. It was three in the morning. I was sitting by a hotel pool in Las Vegas. I was more than slightly buzzed from my texts with Matt. My sense of heightened sexuality was throbbing. I could feel currents of electricity in all the usual places, plus a handful of others, thanks to some lewd suggestions that Matt had texted.

It was true. I was like flotsam on an ocean's current, caught in a temporary eddy but definitely being pulled with the relentless tide. I was resisting, but only halfheartedly.

Hey, what happens in Vegas, stays in Vegas. Right?

My naïveté. My innocence. My small world. All of it was being dismantled piece by piece, like removing individual pieces from a jigsaw puzzle until the picture is not recognizable anymore. Until the picture could be anything.

With each sultry song on my iPod, with each text from Matt, with each lecherous smile from strangers...I was becoming a new person. A desirable person. Not the mother of two children. Not the woman who had suffered through two bouts of colicky babies with spit-up on her sweatshirt in oversized sweatpants.

Not the wife of a good, decent, but uninteresting husband.

Or, maybe more to the point—not the boring wife of a good, decent man.

These thoughts flashed through my mind as this young man continued to stand in front of me, his eyes hungrily scanning my body. I should have been outraged. Or at least shocked. Instead, I was only slightly amused. I was enjoying the attention.

"You're really sexy," he said, blurting out what was apparently in his mind.

I smiled sweetly. "Thank you. That's very nice to hear." What?! Who *is* this person talking this way?

We chatted for a couple of minutes. I felt silly but, at the same time, completely comfortable. Like I was an actress in a play she'd never imagined herself in.

"You want to dance?" he asked, nodding toward the poolside speakers that were playing incredibly loudly for this time of the morning.

He reached his hand toward me. I started to reach for it, thinking, "Why not?" But then, the Melissa I have always been returned and assumed her place front and center. I smiled. "Thank you, but no."

A last shot, he nodded toward my gin and tonic. "Can I get you another?"

I shook my head.

He shrugged and turned away in search of some other prey.

Thank God I still had a few wits about me—even if they were hanging on by a thread. What kind of person allows herself to be flirted with at a Las Vegas pool at three-thirty in the morning? (I did not follow that question with what kind of a person is *at* a Las Vegas pool at three in the morning? That might have thrown me for a loop.)

My insides were afire, alive, yet I was scared to death. I was excited and petrified. There was a huge canyon in front of me. Was I brave enough to leap?

Foolish enough?

By day four, I was like a caged animal, pacing in the SaraBear booth. I probably looked like a crack addict. I was exhausted; my eyes were red-rimmed. I was tapping my feet, twitching my fingers, and constantly checking my phone. My nerves were frayed.

"Sit down," Andrea said. "You're making me nervous."

But I couldn't sit still. With each hour that passed, hours with no buyers, my heart sank deeper into my chest. With each passing hour, I knew that this was bad. Really, really bad.

It was the final day on the floor, and sales were low.

Andrea and I had poured our hearts into preparing for this show. I had used every ounce of energy to be there and put on an awesome display. Our booth itself weighed just under a thousand pounds. If you've never seen the setup and teardown of a trade show floor, you've never seen one of the more remarkable things in life.

The day before a show opens, the vendors arrive at the venue to find their wooden crates plopped in their allocated spot. That's it. Just a shell and crates. A sprawling mess.

At 4:00 a.m. on the opening day of the show, I had headed to the convention center with my large coffee, eyes squinty, hair in a ponytail. The wooden panels of my SaraBear booth were heavy, but thankfully all intact. Somehow, someway, I managed to set this baby up by myself year after year, clicking and locking the large pieces into place. I then carefully, methodically arranged the caddies and our marketing materials in hopes of attracting as many looks—and buyers—as possible.

When it was done, it looked good. Real good. Professional.

The previous year, I had buyers and people coming up to the booth on the last day of the show, paying cash for the diaper caddies that were on display. They were snatching up the demos! They wanted them, loved them!

With the previous year in mind, I'd shipped extra, thinking I'd be prepared and sell them at the booth.

But this year was not last year. We sold a handful for cash but rather than pay to ship the rest back to NY, I threw them away or donated them. Each one, more money down the toilet. The tens of thousands of dollars it cost to come to the trade show could not be recouped without sales. And without buyers stopping by, there were no sales.

I was in a black mood when the show closed. Andrea, to her good fortune, got out early, having left for her flight—as planned—toward the end of the last day.

"You sure you don't want me to reschedule my flight?" she asked. I could hear in her voice the unstated plea, "No, no, no!"

I shook my head. It would only cost more money to rebook her flight and get another ticket. Besides, she was only asking to be polite. I knew that. Even in my fog, I knew that she was trying to be nice. I had lost all patience with her, but I could still recognize that.

There was still enough of me left for that.

Once she was gone, I was left alone, sitting on the wooden bar stool in the middle of the booth, in shock.

I buried my head in my hands. "Fuck me," I whispered to myself. "Fuck me, fuck me, fuck me."

Despite the offer to fly home with Matt, I ended up flying home alone. I was numb. My right wrist and hand were wrapped in gauze, cut up from tearing down and packing the SaraBear display myself. All I could see was darkness ahead. Gloom. The end. There was only a small, flickering light. A small hope.

A desperate chance.

I still had Matt's number.

Chapter 14
LEAP OF UNFAITH

Bob Dylan sings, "Time is a jet plane; it moves too fast." No kidding. Nothing made me understand how deeply that line cuts as arriving back in New York. Six hours earlier, I was in Las Vegas with my life balanced on the head of a pin. Who was I? Should I—would I—have an affair? But here I was, back in the same old house. Hi, kids. Hey, Benny.

I could practically *taste* the spice of life.

Now I was back to ground beef and ketchup.

I was physically home. But mentally, emotionally, spiritually—in every other way—I was someplace far, far away. In New York, I was going through the motions. All I could concentrate on was thoughts of Matt and how to save SaraBear.

The days blended one into another after I got back. I remember Benny telling me that I had to eat something, but I don't recall eating a thing. The weight melted off me. My phone became an appendage more dear to me than my hands. I was beginning to look like a strung-out crack whore.

What if Matt called? I had to make sure that Ben didn't see *that* phone call! But then, what if he *didn't* call? I couldn't bear to think of that possibility. The bad habit that had come back for a cameo appearance in my life in Las Vegas was sticking around. I was drinking. A lot. Vodka and gin had become my poisons of choice.

By five every evening, I was deep into the drink. By midevening, I might just as well have been in Vegas. I could close my eyes, put on music, and think I was poolside again, teetering on the precipice but not yet falling over.

My days were harsh and bleak. I went to the SaraBear office downtown. Day after day, I was faced with the ugliest of realities. Things were really, genuinely collapsing. It was happening in slow motion. I could see each and every pressure point, each and every seam bursting apart…just like I could feel my soul both imploding and exploding at the same instant.

The days took on a surreal regularity. Everything was so fucked!

"Come on, God. It's me. Melissa. Help me out here. I'm drowning!" I prayed as fervently as I'd ever prayed during my mom's illness. I needed a sign. I needed an answer. I felt like a hamster running on his circular wheel, racing around and around, trying to get somewhere but getting nowhere.

And all the time, I was keeping up "appearances." When the tenants next door popped in to say hello, I was all smiles and "How's your day going?" But I was collapsing like a cheap house of cards on the inside.

The debt I was buried under! I was hiding the numbers from Benny. Lying to him. Trying to lie to myself. Knowing that there was no future but hoping against hope that there was.

Why couldn't I convince myself that things would be all right? The reasons why were pretty obvious: *three* mortgages on the house, $75,000 of credit-card debt, $120,000 owed to China, and thousands more to other vendors, logistics companies, distributors, the phone company, my accountant, and on and on and on. And the bottom falling out on sales.

The waiting game I was in for the net-sixty days that arrived net-ninety late told me that time was running out.

Waiting for checks to arrive from Target wasn't paying my bills.

By November 2008, even I couldn't escape the reality. The global economic crisis had hit. Objectively, as bad as I was dealing with it, I was probably not a whole lot worse than most people. Everywhere I turned, the mood was nasty. People who had been friendly and helpful became curt. They sounded annoyed. They stopped returning calls. They stopped returning emails. Checks stopped coming in from stores. Invoices came quicker from vendors.

I was frustrated. I was outraged. Stores weren't paying. There was no money coming in, and there was nothing I could do about it. Things were going downhill...fast. SaraBear was hanging on by a thread.

My "moment of Zen" or hope was when, every evening, I would sneak away and call or text Matt. Sometimes he was there; other nights he was silent. But during those evenings, I was pulled inexorably toward a different life. Whether in a week or a month, it didn't matter. Soon after returning to New York, the die had been cast. I knew—*he* knew—what would happen. We were playing out roles, just as they had been played out since the beginning of time.

Looking back, I only wish I had been unique. Instead, I just allowed myself to be drawn into a tawdry affair.

Two weeks after returning to New York, I found myself sitting in my parked car, tapping my foot, nervous and unbearably excited, looking at a fairly nondescript hotel. I wasn't thinking of my husband or my children. I was thinking if Matt would like the underwear I had on.

I knew what I was doing was wrong. God, I wish I could say I didn't. But I did. What was worse, over the weeks of speaking to and texting Matt, I also had his true measure. He was no knight on a white steed come to rescue me from my life or my financial straits. He was a con artist, a man out for himself, and I knew it.

I chose to ignore it. Instead, I chose to focus on the cut of my panties and how I would look the first time he saw me in them.

I did not think at that moment, sitting in the car, aware that this was my last chance to turn back, that I was the embodiment of what desperation looked like. Looking back, seeing myself in the car...God, I was desperate. Desperate for something, anything that would make the horror of what I'd made of my life seem bearable.

In my desperation he just seemed so much larger than life. He was gorgeous. He was mysterious and intriguing. He had money, or so he let on. He knew people who could help me, or so he suggested.

I saw the black Mercedes glide into the parking lot. Saw him get out and walk toward the hotel lobby. I drew a deep breath and then, with my last chance to turn back, I opened the car door, stepped out, and with my head down, as not to make eye contact with another soul, I followed him in.

***

Of course, if I had been cold to Benny before, I was avoiding him like the plague now. If he went into one room, I went into another. Whenever I could, I would get out of the house after dinner, leaving Ben with the kids. I would just drive and drive for hours. Listening to music. Letting my thoughts drift. Just killing time while I waited for Matt to text or call.

This was my world for a month, maybe two. Then, suddenly one evening I couldn't get through to Matt. When I called his phone number, I got a message that the number had been disconnected. My texts came back "return to sender." That was sweet, having to stare at my words thrown back at me like that. Reading my desperation.

"Where the fuck are you?" I texted into the ether.

Of course, I was so consumed with my own world, wants, and failings that I didn't realize that even as he had been engaged in an affair with me, Matt was losing thousands, if not millions, of dollars in the stock market. His Benz was getting repossessed. His world was crumbling. Everyone's world was crumbling. *The* world was crumbling.

But none of this entered my consciousness. Not then.

All I knew was rejection. I couldn't get what I needed, whatever that was. I had been meandering toward this for the last few years. Sometimes haltingly. Sometimes directly. But I had finally reached the end of the road, and I came face to face with the darkness. Check. Mate.

I can't do this. I can't do this. I can't do this. I can't...

What can't I do?

Keep up with my life? Deal with the rejection? Or finally be done with all of it?

Everything was too much, just too much.

"I can't," I told myself. I was standing in the kitchen. I glanced over at the doorway and saw my kids watching television. I blinked away some tears. I poured a vodka tonic and downed it like water. Then another. And another.

The kids were still watching television. A cartoon, I think.

After the fourth vodka tonic, I started to cry. Tears just rolled down my cheeks. My thoughts filled with the insurmountable debt that had become our life. *I just can't do this anymore.* I braced my hands on the kitchen counter. I started to reach for the vodka to pour another. But then I stopped. I whisked the bottle off the counter and headed for the garage. I sat down behind the wheel of my SUV. I was crying hard. Bawling.

I lifted the bottle and began to chug, the vodka going down in disgust. I did not know what the answer was, but at that moment the only words in my head were "If there *is* an answer, it is definitely at the bottom of this bottle. I know it. Come on, get me to the bottom. There's light there. There's gotta be help there..."

So there I was, standing at the proverbial cliff.

And I jumped. Chasing relief. Chasing an answer. Chasing away the feeling of rejection.

"Mom?"

"Mommy, where are you?"

Oh my God. My kids. I could hear them yelling from inside the house. *I can't do this. I can't...*

I reached for my cell phone. For the first time in a long time, I wasn't looking for Matt's number. It was Benny I was calling.

"Benny, you have to come home. I can't...I can't take care of the kids."

His voice was tight and direct. I could hear his concern. "Are you OK?"

I shook my head. "No. No, I'm not. You have to come home right away. I need you to come home. I can't do it anymore..."

"Calm down, Melissa. I will be there as soon as I can."

The next thing I knew for certain was that Ben was home. I was a disgusting, blubbering mess. I was sobbing. Begging him to forgive me. Saying I didn't deserve to go on. That I'd fucked up everything. We were going to lose everything. I had spent all our money.

Benny. Strong, calm, conventional Benny. He looked at me and listened with some alarm, keeping things under control for the kids. "Mommy just doesn't feel good right now. It's going to be OK."

I shook my head. *It's not. It's not.*

"Do you want me to take you to the hospital?"

I nodded. "Yes. Yes."

I. Had. Cracked.

I must have been close to alcohol poisoning, the sheer amount I had consumed. Yet I remember every detail up until the nurse pushed the sedative through the IV line that they had to hold me down to get into my arm. I remember the drive to the ER with the kids in the backseat. I remember Benny talking to the nurse and letting her know why I was there. He glanced back at me, telling the story from the phone call and coming home to find me.

I can't imagine what my poor kids were thinking. To this day, I don't have the heart to revisit that particular chapter in our lives.

As I watched Benny talk to the triage nurse, all of a sudden, I decided I wanted to go home.

"I need to get out of here. Take me home."

"No, Melissa."

I headed for the door, only to have a security guard grab my arm.

"Leave me alone!"

A couple more security guys came over. Suddenly, they were calmly walking me into the ER, away from my children's view, into a room. I began to fight, kicking and screaming. I recall Benny standing in the door with a frightened look on his face. The corners of his mouth fell down with sadness. There was disgust in his eyes.

They strapped me down with thick, leather belts. A nurse, moving as quickly as I've ever known anyone to move, established an IV line in my arm.

The sedative was pushed.
And that was it: lights out.

I was desperate to pee. The sensation woke me up what must have been hours later. "Where am I?" I wondered. It took a moment for me to remember, but then it all came back. I looked at the IV drip in my arm. I tried to assess how I felt. Physically, I felt remarkably good. Calm. They must have sedated me. But psychologically, I was dazed and confused. Empty.

The room was dark and shadowy, but there was a light on in the hallway. I didn't know, but it seemed to be late at night. Just then, a woman with sensible shoes and an outdated wool blazer came into my room. She paused to look at me and then smiled sweetly and condescendingly.

"Melissa?"

"Yes?"

"How are you?"

"I really have to pee."

She smiled again. "I'll get a nurse to help you with that in a second." She came closer to the bed. "Do you want to stay, Melissa?"

I focused on her face: plain but not unattractive. I couldn't figure out how old she was. Older than me, but not nearly my mom's age. I drew a breath and then nodded.

"Is that a yes?"

I nodded again. "Yes. I need a rest. I need help. I can't go home."

A short time later, I found myself in a unit of the hospital I'd never seen before. Here, the doors are locked from both sides. The walls are white. There are no sharp objects. Eating utensils are plastic, and the plates are paper.

The room I was assigned was as one would expect in the loony bin. There was a bed under a bolted window, a pillow, one blanket, and a white towel on the plastic chair. I lay down on the bed, and at that moment I felt hollowed out like a gutted deer. Like a corpse. A shell of a person. A body with no soul. Yet, I was so remarkably relieved to be there.

Hollow. That's the best I can describe the next thirty-six hours. I slept a lot. I'd wake up to pee. Then I'd sleep some more. When someone asked if I wanted to eat, I said, "No." When someone asked if I wanted to participate in a group session, I politely and softly said, "No thank you."

I slept.

When I woke up, I barely noted the changes in the sky outside the window. Day. Evening. Night. Morning. I slept. In silence. Curled into a ball. So comfortable. So safe. I could not imagine any place in the world I would rather have been. My thoughts were empty. Just empty seconds drifting into empty minutes and hours. One after another. No thoughts. No worries.

And for thirty-six hours…I slept.

By Sunday, my brain cells were starting to come back to life and reconnect. Like wisps of clouds, thoughts and sensations were drifting through my mind. I felt hungry. Famished, actually. I wanted a turkey sandwich and a ginger ale.

I tried to sort out what day it was and how long I'd been there. Without having a clear sense of time, I had to ask one of the nurses.

"It's Sunday morning at eleven," she said. "Sunday?" I thought. I'd been there since Friday night. I had to get sorted out. I got out of bed and made my way to the pay phone on the wall at the end of the hall. As I did, I felt like I'd landed myself in a scene from *One Flew Over the Cuckoo's Nest*. I mean, people were wandering the halls, mumbling to themselves—or to people only they could see—keeping their eyes down. They were all disheveled, and they all looked and acted bat-shit crazy. Even worse, the place smelled like an revolting blend of floor cleaner/cafeteria food/urine/body odor. It was nauseating.

There was no question about the number I was going to dial.

"Benny," I said when he answered. "Get me out of here."

"I can't. Not yet."

Not yet? Why not? As I continued to come back to earth and my synapses started firing in a logical manner, I looked around and came to the firm conclusion that I didn't belong here.

"Jesus H. Christ," I thought to myself. "These people are *crazy*!"

OK, I knew I had stretched way too thin and that I'd snapped, but I wasn't crazy. I needed some rest. I needed sleep. I needed a little detox. But these people were frigging psychotic.

Not me.

"Nurse," I said, grabbing the first one that passed my way.

"Yes?"

"Can I go home now?" I asked politely, adding a smile.

The nurse returned my smile. "No, Melissa. You won't be discharged until you've been evaluated and cleared by a psychiatrist."

How'd she know my name?

I got the picture fast. She didn't have to tell me twice. Good behavior. Playing by the rules. Not being crazy. Those were the ways to get out of that hellhole. So, I did exactly what I was told, and I did all of it.

Over the course of the next two days, I had a single goal, and it was to get myself out of there. So, I played along. I went to every meeting I was told to attend—and I participated. I ate with others using my plastic silverware in the dining room. I spoke earnestly to the therapist assigned to my case.

No other actress has given as Oscar-worthy a performance as I did for those twenty-four hours. I spoke my lines perfectly, with feeling and emotion. I showered. I stayed alert. I told them I thought I was capable of continuing my therapy at home.

Honest.

So, after my determined effort, they let me go. But only into Benny's close care and strict supervision.

Deal! Give me meatloaf! Get me out of this fucking nut house!

Matt, of course, was completely out of the picture. For all he knew, I was dead. Hell, for all I knew, he was dead. That sordid chapter had come to a close. I was in the house with Benny and my children.

Benny was amazing. He was attentive. He cooked. He cleaned. He took care of the kids. But it was too late for me and him. I had a wall up—a wall that I had been building brick by brick for a long time, long before Matt came into the picture.

The wall was solid and impenetrable. Nothing short of an explosion would tear it down now.

Chapter 15

OUR DOG IS DEAD, AND SO IS OUR MARRIAGE

My only concern now was spending time with my children: caring for them, playing with them, loving them. And getting myself well.

I had essentially walked away from SaraBear. On a conscious move, I closed the office. Didn't answer the phone. Didn't return emails. I had become like everyone else. It was more than I could deal with, so I just walked away. I washed my hands of anything and everything SaraBear for three weeks. My life was about caring for my kids, spending time with them, making them meals, taking walks together, going for drives. In between, I slept and cleaned.

Finally, in early December, I went back to the office to "assess the damage."

The office was cold and quiet. There was no life. I walked around the space, finding it to be both familiar but so alien at the same time, like a place I'd once visited in another life. I sat down at my desk chair and swiveled it this way and that. Then I leaned back and put my hands behind my head.

With my brain thoroughly cleansed of alcohol and forcefully purged of the infatuation with Matt, a strategy began to form in my mind. In a final attempt to make my eight-hundred-pound gorilla, pain-in-the-ass, I've-riddled-my-family-with-debt business succeed, which I had started and then lived and breathed for so long, I decided to completely restrategize. From top to bottom. What had I done right? What had I done wrong? What did I need to do now? So I sat there for two hours and mapped out a plan. At this point, I had nothing to lose and only everything to gain.

I was as hardnosed and calculating as any other CEO. Boutiques, screw you. You don't pay anyway. I'm not shipping you six goddamn caddies at a time. FedEx, screw you too. You're a pain to do business with and really expensive. Dear warehouse, you'll get your money when I ship shit out, and not one second before. China…hmm, China. Don't want to anger China too much. China, please give me sixty more days to pay. Please.

Mr. Factor, how about an advance on the guarantee of a huge Target order in the spring? Target, I love you and your orders. Here's the deal. Give us orders, and we'll ship. Whatever you want, we'll deliver. Babies "R" Us, pay attention now. Target loves the diaper caddy. You will too. Let's talk.

My brutal assessments and actions weren't limited to corporations and nations. I fired Andrea that day. Sorry, but I'm paying you off my credit card, and you don't equate to sales. Then I shut down and cleaned out the office. SaraBear was coming back home again.

I also knew that, at least in the short term, there was no way I could rely only on SaraBear as a revenue stream. I needed income. I needed a cash flow. I needed a job.

When I walked away from nursing in order to focus exclusively on SaraBear, I swore to myself that I would never again work a job where I had to clock in and clock out, where I couldn't call my own shots. But there I was, desperate. So, with my proverbial tail between my legs, I went back to the hospital.

And they took me back!

When I was young and girls were told to become secretaries or nurses to have a skill and a trade that they could "fall back on," I didn't pay much attention. Becoming a nurse then hadn't been a strategy. It was what I thought I wanted.

But I found out only too clearly that it is a good thing to have something "to fall back on." Want to be a dancer? Learn a trade as well. Want to sing and act on Broadway? Learn to do something other than waiting tables. Dreamers who follow their dreams have to be smart and calculating. Just like entrepreneurs. There's way more failure than success, way more hurt than healing. Whether you want to start a business, or be a star, or a great athlete, you have to be prepared for the hard times. The hard times will help make you an even greater success.

It didn't feel like a step toward success when I went back to the hospital to get my job back. It didn't feel like a step toward success when I faked smiles and took good care of my patients. It didn't feel like a step toward success when I hid the hole in my soul.

But it was.

My nursing degree let me find my bearings again. I was thankful, yet embarrassed, to have returned. But it gave me something to do, money coming in, and a chance to exist outside of SaraBear. I needed all those things.

So there I was, cleaned out. Fresh. Day after day, I felt some semblance of control return. So then I just hunkered down and waited. The boutiques were pissed, just like I expected them to be. Too bad. They weren't going to save me. I knew what had to happen: it was all about Target. So. I waited for their spring orders.

In a couple of months, strategy and patience started to pay off. By April, Target orders were flying out the door. Money was coming in again. SaraBear floundered, but it didn't sink. My book keeper, Kim, and I got together every few weeks to decide who got paid that month and who didn't get paid for another month.

Along the way, I gradually became a master of buying time, negotiating and renegotiating terms, and managing calls and emails. A Zen master.

There was an added benefit to the laser-like focus I had to apply to keep SaraBear afloat. It helped me get my mind back. I was regaining control of my business and my life. I'd been in therapy from the time I got out of the loony bin. I'd managed to stop drinking.

I was changing. It was almost like I could feel my own self growing back.

Benny was changing too. That was good. What wasn't good was that we weren't changing together. Our changes were pulling us even farther apart. The train track had split, and we were on separate cars.

I was headed one way; he was headed another. I knew it, and I think he knew it too. I was resigned, almost welcoming of that reality. He wasn't.

Meanwhile, SaraBear was not just surviving but was starting to thrive month to month. I was hearing rumors from my rep that BRU wanted the product in the fall. All good. Things were really starting to improve now.

The dark cloud was Ben. He was becoming moodier. He would have dark times, times when he would get very angry at me. Now that I was getting healthy again and he didn't have to walk on eggshells around me, his resentment of how I'd sucked the life out of the family was exploding into full view.

He'd had enough: enough of me, of the business, of the wall I'd put between us.

We were arguing constantly. Sometimes we argued about things worth arguing about. Mostly we argued just because we'd lost the ability to interact any other way.

The endings were always ugly. Ugly and sad.

While all this was going on, Tommy, the golden retriever we'd had and loved for eleven years, was coming to his last happy days with us. Tommy. Sweetest dog ever. His old body was just beat. He was tired. Every morning, Tommy walked with me and the kids to the end of the driveway to meet the school bus. This particular Thursday, he walked down with the kids, but he couldn't walk back. His legs just didn't have it in them. They'd stopped working.

"Oh, Tommy, my old friend." I lifted him up and carried him back to the house, where he rested.

The next evening Ben lifted Tommy into the truck, and we drove him to the vet. His final car ride. It's a horrible thing to have to put down a dog like Tommy. He meant everything to us. He'd been there with us for everything, the good and the bad, the high and the low. As he lay in our arms on the floor, wrapped in his favorite blanket, our golden retriever companion, peacefully and calmly, took his last breath.

Holding his limp body, Benny and I cried. We cried for Tommy, sure. But we cried for so much more. We had lost more than Tommy, and holding him in our arms just made that so real. Our first baby, Tommy, had been with us since the beginning of our relationship. He was our first responsibility together and represented the length of time we had been together. And to let him go was an end of an era.

When we finally left Tommy at the vet, I looked at Benny from the passenger side of the car. "I can't go home to the kids just yet."

"Me either," he said.

So we drove around until we ended up in the parking lot of the local park where our kids play. The moon had come out. It was night. We just sat there, staring straight ahead, not talking. So close together and so hopelessly far apart.

I was crying. I just couldn't stop crying.

"Benny?"

"Yes?"

Staring straight ahead, tears flowing down my cheeks, I said in a voice barely above a whisper, "I can't be who you need me to be. I can't. I just can't."

There was quiet for a moment, the most heart-wrenching quiet I have ever known. Then he drew a soft breath. "I know, Melissa. I know."

There. It was said. The weight that had been dragging us down was finally acknowledged. We both knew it was there, but until we said it, and said it to one another, it couldn't be freed. And neither could we. It was terribly sad and terribly true. It was a lot of things. It wasn't easy. Life was awkward and raw those next few months. For a lot of it, we went through the motions. Business, marriage, work, daycare, kids. We worried about the kids. And then there were the practicalities of what lay ahead. Who will move out? Who will stay? What—and how—will we tell the kids?

How does one *do* this?

Finally, after more nasty fights than I care to count, we decided that I should leave the house. It was the right decision. The house had always meant more to Benny than to me. Besides, if he was to move, it would have created all sorts of practical complications that we didn't need. Unlike me, he couldn't move out of the county because of his job. He had to stay put.

It was just fortuitous that a friend of mine had a vacant house that I could stay in that was only a short distance away.

Once all that was decided, we decided on a day. When we first settled on the day I would move out, it seemed a long way away. An eternity. But then, day by day, it snuck up on me.

It was time.

I opened my closet door. I could hear the kids' voices as they played in the living room. Laughing. Giggling. Without a clue that their world was about to change forever. God, I wished I could change everything.

But I couldn't.

So I just steeled myself and dragged the huge, ugly green suitcase from the back of the closet. I pulled it up onto the bed. Then I went through my drawers, throwing my clothes into the suitcase. I stuck all my toiletries in a tote and shoved it in the suitcase, along with some shoes.

My life. My future. All thrown into that ugly fucking suitcase.

Sara saw me first as I made my way down the stairs. "Where are you going, Mom?"

I smiled bravely. "Oh, just to Christy's house for a few days. Mommy needs a little break, honey." I looked over to Benny, hoping for a little bit of support, if only for the kids' sake. But I wasn't going to get it. He wasn't giving ground on this one. Maybe he understood that we had reached this place where we had to end it, but he was damned sure that it wasn't his fault that we'd gotten here. He had been good, steady, decent, conventional—everything he was raised to be.

It wasn't his fault that that was the exact opposite of what I needed right then.

So, as I lugged my suitcase toward the door and Sara stopped me to ask where I was going, Ben stood in the kitchen in front of the sink with his arms crossed and legs spread apart in his police-officer stance. Cold eyes. Jaw clenched. I know Benny. This was taking all his emotional strength. He's a good man. This was a failure he was taking very personally.

He shouldn't have. It was my failure.

I dragged the suitcase out the door. There was no net to catch me now. My kids were hurt and confused. I was leaving my home with nothing but a suitcase of crappy clothes and the very real possibility of financial ruin.

But if I could just hold it together, I knew things weren't as bad as they seemed. Yes, my marriage was over. But that happened to people all the time. My kids were confused and hurt, but I knew they'd be OK. And I would get my shit together and make it right.

The future wasn't rosy, but it wasn't all that bleak either. Target was ordering, and the money was coming in. If that would only continue, things would be fine.

When I got to Christy's house, my footsteps echoed in the empty house. No family there. No laughter. No warmth. Just a safe sanctuary, even if I didn't feel safe at all.

I don't remember those first few hours in the barren house. I don't know where I put the suitcase, or whether I splashed my face or had a drink of water. I don't know whether I checked the kitchen to see if there was anything in the cupboards.

I don't know if I walked through the house, opening closet doors, getting familiar with the place. The only thing I remember clearly was finding myself flat on my back on the bed in the master bedroom, staring up at the ceiling. I was numb. In shock.

Over the next few days and weeks, I stared at that ceiling a lot. It became like a reflected map of my soul. It looked fine at first glance, maybe a little tired and in need of a fresh coat of paint, but fine nonetheless.

But then, the more you looked, you could begin to see cracks in the plaster. Some wider than others. Some definitely in need of patching.

You could see discoloration. If you looked closely, you could see a spider web in the far corner. You could see the collection of small bugs in the light fixture.

You could see that it wasn't all that "all right" at all.

And I just lay there, noting this weird topography, knowing that what I was seeing was really just me.

I felt numb. I would not say I was depressed. I didn't feel sad. I didn't feel particularly lost.

I just felt numb.

And deep inside of me, there was a part of me that was starting to fight, a part of me that wasn't satisfied with just being numb. She was awakening.

Chapter 16
SHOCK AT 200 JOULES

How the fuck did I get here? When did I become the poster girl for "not the life I ever thought I would be living"?

There was another question that tormented me during this particular stretch in my life, a question that would present itself to me at all hours of the day or night, in my dreams, when I was sitting on the porch, staring out into space, and while I was shopping. The question was who *are* you?

It was a question that I couldn't answer. Even during my lowest moments in the house I shared with Benny, I thought I could answer that question. I was a wife and mother. I was a young woman trying to fit into a life. But now? I *did* some of these things still, but the role didn't seem to fit the same way. The one thing I cherished in my life, the one thing that gave me joy despite the challenges and difficulties, was being a mother to my children. But now, I wasn't even living in the same house with them. I felt that that small beam of grace was gone from me as well.

There was, however, a tremendous sense of relief.

I was trying, goddammit; I was trying to find a way. I didn't know who I was, but I was getting more and more interested in finding out. So, even as that question filtered through my mind over the next few months, I tried to find some semblance of "normal" to call my own, but it didn't come easy. Once the numbness finally started to seep away, I felt a lot of things. Normal wasn't one of them. Mostly I felt guilt.

What had I done? Who *was* I?

SaraBear had made me a balance sheet genius. During this time, I was totaling up things more complicated than dollars and cents. My failures kept adding up, beyond anything I was able to fathom. They were beyond my ability to feel.

But even at my lowest point, I was not a victim. I might not have known the answer to who I was, but I sure as hell knew how I'd gotten here. I'd made the choices. I'd marked the path. I'd set my sights on a horizon that I hadn't yet reached.

It was my dream. My desire. My passion.

It was me.

I know there are people who would see in my desire something noble, something almost poetic. I would remind them to remember there is always a whole life to weigh and the lives of others as well. I would ask them to hear the choked, angry voice of my husband—yes, still my husband—as he reminded me how I was pretty much a whore and that I'd ruined his life and my children's lives as well.

I wish I had a good argument.

I didn't care so much about his bruising criticism of me. It hurt, but I was beyond the sharpness of feeling for that. It was only my kids that made me feel. And his criticism about what I'd done to them cut me deeply.

And it rang true.

In the neighborhood, I understood what it must have been like for Hester Prynne in *The Scarlet Letter*. To say that what happened rocked our neighborhood would be an understatement. No one, not one person who knew us, would have pegged Benny and me to be the ones to split up.

Or for me to walk out.

No one saw it coming because I kept my life quiet and private. My struggles were well hidden.

I felt their eyes on me.

"She did *what?*"

"She left him."

Why? Why? Why?

We were the perfect middle-America couple. Cop and nurse. White picket fence. Two perfect children. A dog and a cat.

"Splitsville."

"Are you sure? Where is she living?"

Whisper. Whisper.

I will say one thing: whatever else I'd managed to do, I had managed to change the recipe of my life. I never thought I'd be where I was. Never.

What happened to that middle American mom, filled with frustration? What happened to my Main Street USA life? Sure, I'd pushed the boundaries a bit. I'd taken on my own business. And SaraBear was a friggin' demon. But, at base, I was still me. A wife and a mother.

Now?

OK, the wife part was definitely shot to hell. But that was OK. I could live without that. Hell, I could probably thrive without it. But the mom thing? That hurt. That was cutting like a sharp knife.

"How come you don't sleep at home, Mommy?"

My just-starting-to-feel-things-again heart just about broke when Nathan asked me that. So little. So sweet. My little boy. Sara was clearly done with me. She was really not interested in talking to me at all. When she was with me, she tended to fold her arms at me a lot and huff impatiently, gestures that I found to be remarkably like those her father was capable of employing. Still, I didn't think I had any right to take issue with her…or with Benny either, for that matter.

I accepted that everything that had gone wrong was my fault. All of it. I was the one who had fucked up.

"It *isn't* all your fault," Kim insisted, leaning toward me as we sat across from each other at her kitchen table.

"What am I going to do?" I asked her, my bookkeeper and my friend. My *only* friend. She was my supporter and best cheerleader.

"What do you want to do?"

I stared at her blankly. Was she crazy? Did I have a choice? Then I sipped my iced tea. Looking away, I sighed. "I want to make it all right,"

I confessed. "I want my kids to love me again instead of hate me." I tried to keep my voice from breaking. "I want to end the marriage and still be friends with Benny."

She sighed and leaned back. "OK. Tall order, but OK."

Then I looked her in the eye. "And I want to keep SaraBear afloat."

She smiled. "You're tenacious, I'll give you that."

I nodded. "How bad is it?"

She looked at me as my bookkeeper. "You ready?"

I nodded.

"Not great," she began gently. She then walked me through the financial disaster that SaraBear had become.

Meanwhile, the kids really didn't like coming to my house. "My" house. That still felt funny saying. It was rough for me, and it had to be hard for them. But, hey, they're kids. They're resilient. Their world changed, but it didn't break. Their dad still loved them. I still loved them. Things changed. Serious things changed. Scary things. Their world shook, but the center managed to hold. Over time, the difficult questions slowed and then stopped, and they just became used to this new arrangement.

It became "normal" for them.

Slowly, it became normal for me as well. As my nerve endings started to come out of their slumber, I began to get used to this "new" Melissa. Even though I continued to be pretty dulled to most things, my joy with my children came intensely to life. Blossomed in a way it never had. I was completely and totally engaged in being all the mother I could be.

The more time I spent with them, the more I realized that even when I had been living in the same house with them, I hadn't been *with* them. My mind had been someplace else. Or I was drinking. I was never really *engaged*.

No more.

When I was with them, now, I was really *with* them. Completely and totally present. They filled my entire space. When I was with my kids, I wasn't on the computer; I wasn't on my phone; I wasn't staring into

Recipe for Disaster

space; I wasn't focused on my own psychic pain, thinking of my next move, my next task, my next step in my avoidance dance with Benny.

I was present with them and in their little, beautiful, precious lives.

We would sit on the floor and play games. Games! And I played with them. Yahtzee. Chutes and Ladders. Candy Land. Any game they wanted to play, we played. We lay in bed together. In *my* bed. No rules about children not being allowed! In my bed, my children were welcome! Just to sit or to sleep with me. To cuddle. Goof. Laugh. Twirl our hair. We would watch television cuddled under the blankets.

How I expected the thunder to roll and the lightning to crack when I broke *those* two rules! Imagine, watching television in my bed with my kids! It was glorious!

One thing I did find was my voice…that still-prayerful voice within me. I prayed a lot during that time, mostly for my kids to be able to love their mother in a new, real light. I wanted them to see me as strong, as weak, as a whole person. But more than anything, I wanted them to see and feel me as a nurturing mother who loved them more than life itself, a mother who would do anything and everything in her power to make things right and not let them down.

Dammit, I was not going to let my financial crisis destroy their world. I wouldn't.

Slowly, I incorporated work with my life. I had to have an income. I might have had to force myself to do it, but at least I had something I could do. And working as a nurse allowed me to keep my life somewhat balanced as I tried to continue to keep the train on the tracks of life.

Anyone who's ever watched "Nurse Jackie" would have a good idea of what I was like as a nurse—only, instead of drugs, I was ducking into the locker room, or the bathroom, or the lunchroom, to check my Blackberry and keep up with SaraBear. Maybe I went down for the count, but SaraBear hadn't. Not yet. It needed some TLC, some intensive medical attention, but it hadn't reached the end of its life yet. There were still Target orders to fill. The manufacturer in China was still assembling thousands and thousands of caddies. I had to negotiate with the freight forwarder that was handling containers coming into the port of Los Angeles.

Cracking up. Being a nurse. Being a mother. None of that changed those responsibilities. I was going to dig myself and my family out from under the financial weight I'd created. Most of my nurse friends were dogged tired by their shifts. Me, my day still began at four in the morning. I caught up on what I needed to know for SaraBear. Then I got ready for the "real" day. Kids went off to school and daycare, and I went to "work." Then I picked up the kids and took them to whatever afterschool activity they had. Dinner and time devoted to them. Then it was back to SaraBear until bedtime.

The sense of numbness was falling away from me each day. I was feeling more alive. I was exhausted, annoyed, frustrated, overjoyed, beaten down, and raised up each day. Through it all, I kept focused on SaraBear. SaraBear had gotten me into the mess I was in, but it could get me out too.

Sales of the caddy had still been strong at Target. We were meeting or exceeding projections every week. They had bumped up the caddies to more stores. It was now in-line at over seven hundred stores in the United States.

"Just tell me what you need," I emailed my Target rep. "Eight hundred stores? Nine hundred? One thousand?"

Not only was Target going well, I was hearing a buzz that BRU really wanted the product. My BRU rep had emailed a few weeks earlier saying, "Melissa, the buyer, she really likes the SaraBears. Wants to expand the product line. What are your capabilities?" They just had to wait for some store changes to complete before picking up new product lines. But it all looked good.

"Come on, come on..."

The key to everything was selling those damned caddies! If Target bumped it up to one thousand stores, if BRU picked them up...My financial mess could be well on the way to being straightened out.

The sun was shining. The future looked bright. I was just getting a little antsy for it to *get here*!

Mid-October. I was at work at the hospital and finishing up with a patient, putting in and taping up her IV line. "There you go, dear,"

I said, smiling at a sweet, older woman who was soon to have a heart catheterization. "Lunch," I said, walking past the charge nurse. She hardly glanced up. I went outside to feel the sun on my face. As soon as I stepped outside, I checked my email. Nothing. I paced a bit before coming back in to have something to eat.

I stopped by my locker to put away my bag before coming off lunch. I glanced up at the clock. I had to get back to the unit and my patients. I checked my email one more time. There was an unread email from my Target rep.

"It looks as though the buyer has decided to not carry the SaraBear line in 2010. I'm asking for an urgent meeting, but thought you should know for PO projections."

And with those two sentences, my world stopped.

I slumped down on one of the benches in the locker room. "Are you fucking kidding me…?"

I blinked my eyes as to clear them and read the email again. Then again after that. I was bent over, like I had a pain in my gut. This was incredible. I read the email again. Un-mother-fucking-believable. It was so unbelievable that I almost had to laugh. I think I did laugh, or maybe it was God again, as I heard a cackling echo off the metal lockers around me.

What else could I do? That one email, those few words, meant that the bottom was dropping out of my life. Without Target, SaraBear was done. And without SaraBear, the Bramlage family had nothing but a shit storm in front of it. Benny's salary and my nursing salary combined couldn't dig us out of this hole, not in fifty years.

I was fucked.

I walked out of that locker room knowing that nothing short of emergency resuscitation was going to save my life now. SaraBear's heart had stopped.

With no other choice but to smile at my patients and give them the best care I knew how, I made my way back to the unit. My own heart and mind were far, far away.

Part IV
Chapter 17
FEELING MY WAY IN THE DARK

One day at a time.

Good advice for a recovering vodka-holic or a wannabe-entrepreneur looking dead on into the abyss. Even without Target, orders weren't stopping until the end of December. There was cash flow until February.

"Come on, BRU," I prayed. "Don't let me down." I was a gambler, kissing the dice. The odds were not, to put it kindly, favorable. But those shitty odds were all I had. "Come on! Double or nothing."

Meanwhile, Kim very kindly but firmly made sure I didn't completely ignore my eight-hundred-pound furry friend. I was up to my eyeballs in debt. The money coming in until February wasn't going to chip away at that debt. It was only going to keep the electricity running.

"What do you think?" I asked Kim.

The expression on her face told me everything I needed to know. "That bad?"

She nodded. "I think you have to serious think about filing."

"Filing?! As in bankruptcy?"

The word was like dead weight in the room. Bankruptcy. An admission of abject failure. Let me tell you, there is one thing about an entrepreneur that separates him or her from everyone else. She is sure, somehow, someway, that she can make it work. Just another day. Just another account.

Bankruptcy means no more days. No more accounts.

Well, sort of. It's like a patient hearing the word "cancer." It doesn't have to be the end of the world, but damn, the word sure makes it seem like it is.

So, I did as she said. I met with the bankruptcy attorney. Going over the entire situation was painful. There really didn't seem to be any way out.

"Is it really hopeless?" I asked.

He shrugged. "It's never hopeless. We're just getting the lay of the land. Let's give it another couple of weeks and see what happens. If nothing changes…" He let the thought hang there. Like a hangman's noose.

Before, the weight of SaraBear failing weighed on me in terms of a vague, frightening financial disaster. But now that disaster had a name, a shape, a realness—which made it both more and less frightening at the same time.

"I can't go bankrupt," I told the attorney.

He smiled a smile he'd probably smiled a thousand times before. "Of course you can," he said simply. "People do it all the time."

Not me, asshole!

Nothing really changed during the next few weeks, so the bankruptcy attorney suggested that I bring Ben in with me the next time we met.

My heart dropped into my stomach. I appreciated the attorney. He was direct, no bullshit. But right then, I hated him. Really hated him. I knew it was pointless to argue. I also knew he was right.

It was time.

Benny was none too pleased to find himself sitting across from a bankruptcy attorney. For the most part, I'd been able to shield the real mess that was SaraBear's finances from him. He knew things were tough. You didn't take out a third mortgage when things were rosy.

But still.

Both Benny and I come from modest backgrounds. Our families paid their bills in full when they were due. Our parents saved plenty for retirement. That was all part of that "meatloaf" inheritance. Straight up. We had been the same way. When we first got married, we had a big jug to put money in. That was our "mad money." If we didn't have enough money in that jug to, say, go to the movies, we didn't go to the movies. We paid cash for groceries and what we didn't have cash for, we didn't get.

Salt of the earth.

Benny had gotten sucked into the whole SaraBear enterprise because of me. I don't know what he was thinking along the way. Maybe he was glad I'd found something that seemed to occupy me. Maybe he really believed I was going to make a ton of money for us. Whatever, he was supportive in every way. He had helped when I needed him to help. And he signed over whatever we had when I needed him to.

But whatever his thinking had been, I was pretty sure he never anticipated finding himself in this office.

I could literally feel the tension coming off his body as he sat in the chair next to me. He was tightly coiled. I could imagine what a prisoner thought when he saw him like that. Calm. Steely. Ready.

But a seething ready. Like "you really don't want to mess with me" ready.

That's how he was. It scared me.

The attorney was very calm and straightforward. He might just as well have been ordering dinner. To him, it was that straightforward.

Not to me. And not to Benny. To us, it was twisted and wrong with overlays of everything that had gone awry in our life together. It was one big fucking molten mess. Twice, the attorney had to stop what he was saying because Ben stood up abruptly and stormed from the room.

The first time, the attorney looked at me as if to say, "What's going on?"

I hunched down in my chair. "He's pretty upset," I said softly.

The attorney nodded.

What I didn't tell him was that Benny's storming out had been an act of supreme control. If he'd stayed, he'd surely have punched a hole in the wall. Or me.

After the second time he'd stormed out and, several minutes later, come back in, the attorney summed up the situation. Nice and tidy. Neat as could be.

To paraphrase: if SaraBear went under, we were fucked.

More specifically, if SaraBear went under, we would lose the house, all of Ben's retirement savings, our stocks, bonds…everything. Every last thing. Even though we'd been separated for several months, we were still legally married, and the business was tied to the secure debt we called "the kids' home."

SaraBear goes under, it's all gone. We'd be left with nothing but the credit rating of a thief.

After an hour of listening to the attorney, the two of us shuffled outside, both stunned, both overwhelmed. I mean, it wasn't like we could hug each other and cry or anything. I'm sure Benny was thinking that meeting me was the worst thing that could ever have happened to him in his life.

We didn't talk. What was there to say? We stood there in the rain, staring at the street and the cars going by, for a few minutes. I kept seeing those cars and thinking everyone in them was going back or forth to some semblance of a perfect life. Quite unlike me, who had entered a level of unimaginable hell. I glanced over at Benny. There were a million things I wanted to say, but I couldn't find even one word to actually speak.

An interesting thought popped into my head as we paused there. Why don't I just take off and jump in front of one of those cars? That would solve everything, wouldn't it? At least my kids would get my life insurance—before I lost that to bankruptcy too. They'd be better off without me. I was a fucking loser.

I was thinking these very happy thoughts when, without even a look in my direction or a good-bye, Benny just walked off. I got it. I mean, he didn't have anything to say either. We weren't even strangers going our separate ways. We were two people who had shared a life that had broken apart. That was bad enough. But the loose ends—namely bankruptcy—were still forcing us to deal with one another.

A minute later, I turned and walked in the opposite direction, heading toward my SUV. I sat behind the wheel, not even bothering to turn the ignition. Not even turning on the radio.

Recipe for Disaster

The rain was pelting down on the roof of the car. The clouds were heavy and dark. The windows were streaked with rain. I leaned forward and pressed my head against the steering wheel. And I started to cry. Really, really cry.

It all hit me then. I had nowhere to go. Nothing to do. I had tried every option. Played every angle. Overturned every stone. Made every phone call. I used every person, every contact, every country, every keystroke on a computer…everything to try and make it work. I'd already had a nervous breakdown—am I allowed two?

"I don't know what to do," I cried, blubbering over and over. "I don't know what to do."

For years now, every man in a suit or a tie had been a potential investor. Every store that carried *anything* baby related was fair game for a cold call. I did it all. All those hours. Years and years of work and struggle. All that energy. And all for nothing.

Nothing.

It was too much to bear.

For an hour, I sat in the parking spot on Main Street, sobbing. Finally, there were just no tears left. I still didn't start up the car though. Before I did that, I had to plot out a path to the nearest bridge that I could drive off. That option still seemed more inviting that dealing with the worry and guilt I felt.

How could one person cause such a mess?

The rain kept coming down, eventually turning to a drizzle. And then, for just a moment, it stopped, and there was a momentary break in the clouds. A glimpse of sunshine. A promise of what the day *could be*. In that moment, I thought of Babies "R" Us.

It was running the table. Double sixes. Four aces.

It was my only hope. It was a stupid hope. It was outlandish. It was doubling down with nothing to back up my bet. It was desperate. Foolish. But it was all I had, and I wasn't quite ready to relinquish it. My one, tiny ray of hope. A thread…a small thread to grasp. If Babies "R" Us came through, and possibly ordered enough product, I could get out of this with my life intact and our finances in place. My God, if this came through, things could be all right. So, with no more tears to shed, no more energy to put anyplace else, I focused on that small ray of hope and swore that as long as a path to survival existed, I would not give up. I swore I would make this hell I'd created for myself and my family right.

Chapter 18

KISMET

Somehow, someway, the business stayed alive. Even now, I'm not sure how this happened. I sure as hell would never have managed it without Kim. Together, we managed to claw our way month by month and dollar by dollar, staying barely afloat.

If I thought I was a money-managing expert when Benny and I would save our spare change in jugs in the house, I soon had a PhD in fiscal affairs. Peter was still paying Paul. The left hand was blind to the right hand. But day by day, month by month, we kept going.

Life is strange, and sometimes the strangeness seems never to end. Just about everything I'd always thought I would be, I wasn't anymore. And how had all this come to pass? Because I'd gotten enraptured by a dream, an image, a brass ring on the merry-go-round. For the life of me, I couldn't remember how it felt to be so numbed by the "meatloaf life" that I was willing to risk it all to chase after an idea, a product.

A dream.

My god, I didn't know anything. If I could do it over again…But the reality is there are no do-overs in life. I'd stood on the edge of a mighty chasm and, out of desperation and hope, certainty and need, I'd leaped. When I leapt, I just assumed that everything else in my life would be all right. I didn't—I couldn't—factor in how my decisions and my actions would affect Benny, or my children. If I thought about it at all, I assumed that what I did would be successful and that life would be *better*.

I never imagined that my dream would drive us to the edge of an abyss, with nothing but bankruptcy and hopelessness awaiting us.

I was still wrestling with the beast that was SaraBear: my simple idea that had blossomed into an enterprise that just about swallowed my life, and everyone in it, whole. Oh, SaraBear. I had to make this all right. I just *had to.*

Babies "R" Us, I need you!

In February 2010, Babies "R" Us took its first shipment. That was a red-letter day to be sure. But Kim and I knew it was way too early to break out the champagne. The gorilla had slimmed down to seven hundred pounds but was still a really big-ass, ugly gorilla. Still, it was *something.* It was a flickering light in the darkness. I was up to my eyeballs in debt, and BRU was the only glimmer of hope I'd had in what seemed like a lifetime or two. I had been dreaming of this BRU deal for so long—praying for it, longing for it—that it was hard to believe that now it was proving to be real.

Still, it was only a crack in the door. This deal wasn't going to be enough to "right the ship," but it was enough to keep us going and start turning things around.

In life and in business, the good things—and bad things—tend to happen in clusters. As BRU started to take shipments, I felt myself finally getting my sea legs. With BRU on board, my business was stabilizing, but even more important to me, I was becoming the mother I'd always dreamed of being, the one I always believed I could be.

Damn. I'd been through fire, but I could feel some cool, fresh air on my face. Nothing in my life had prepared me for what I'd been through, or what I was still going through, but even without knowing it, I had gotten stronger than I'd ever been. I was a person my parents could never have imagined. And, sadly, a woman my mother would never meet.

I'd stared into the abyss, and I was still there to tell about it.

Things were not all right. Not even close. But I *felt* like I'd turned a corner. The BRU shipments gave me something to hang my hat on as I went looking for a buyer—or any kind of help—for SaraBear.

Throughout everything that had happened, I knew in my heart that, with the right management and in the right hands, it would be a success. I still believed in SaraBear. Maybe I hadn't had the skills, the smarts, the experience, or the luck to make it everything it could have been, but goddamn it, I *knew* it was a great, great idea and product. (I know now that what I was feeling was not unique. Everyone who has ever had a dream, who has ever invented a "better mouse trap," has felt like me. Look up "tenacious" in the dictionary, and there will be a picture of an entrepreneur! Of course, there are those who would suggest the same if you looked up "insane.")

At the time, I couldn't be bothered with labels. I had to convince someone with money to see SaraBear the way I did. I needed investors. I needed a buyer. I met with Gerber. I met with investors. I butted my way into talks and meetings with all the juvenile big dogs. I can't say I was received with the enthusiasm I believed I deserved. I was either passed off to low-level people whose job was basically to ignore people like me, or, at best, I came up against mild interest.

There were times when I understood what was meant by being "damned with faint praise" better than anyone who had ever lived. I wanted to shout at those people, "If you think SaraBear is good, then *take it*! Don't just talk! Do something!"

It would have been better if someone had said, "This is a terrible product." Or "this is the worst idea I've ever seen in all my years in juvenile products."

But they didn't. They couldn't. Because they couldn't help but see what I saw; they couldn't help but know what I knew. It was a great product. I just couldn't get it moving forward without more gas in the tank.

Despite the positive movement with BRU, the stress of the debt load was killing me.

I hadn't had a really good night's sleep in like seven years. Two a.m. usually found me wide awake, weighted down with anxiety and fear, caught between getting up and staying in bed. Not that it mattered. No matter where I found myself, I would just cry. Yes, I was strong. Yes, I had learned a lot about myself. Yes, I was becoming the mom I knew I was supposed to be.

But I was still shattered.

I was still panicking in the middle of the night.

I was still teetering on the edge.

When would it ever end?

Goddamn. The truth was I didn't think it would ever end. Part of me tried to resign myself to the reality that *this* was my life. Like someone with cancer, there would never again be a time when I didn't have cancer. Now, there would never again be a time when I was carefree and safe. Never a 2:00 a.m. that would find me sleeping, snug in my bed, safe and sound and content.

But then, just like you never see the bus coming at you with your name on it, you don't always see when good things are coming your way either.

It was late summer 2010. The weather was perfect. The air played on my skin, teasing and sweet. Kim and I had struggled through another day of balancing, juggling, finagling, stressing, and praying for something to turn around. Finally, around five o'clock, Kim put her head down on the desk with a thud. A moment later, she raised it and looked at me. "Let's get a drink," she said. "I'm done."

"Don't have to ask me twice," I said, sighing with relief.

It was one of those days when, if you were still in school, you begged the teacher to have class outside. The evening, still light with the ending of the day, was so nice it was hard not to feel hopeful.

Even though I had very little to feel hopeful about.

Kim hooked her arm in mine, and together we walked down the street. We passed a couple of stores where we stopped to look in the window, pointing out this dress, or that blouse or those pair of shoes.

"You'd look great in those," I said, nodding in the direction of a strappy pair.

She laughed. "Hell, I'd look so good in those I'd get arrested."

I laughed back. I could tell that Kim was in a mood, and it was all good. Whatever else happened, work and worries could be left far behind.

I don't know if it was the weather or Kim's infectious mood; maybe it was just the sheer physical delight of strolling along the street like a teenager, elbows locked, with a girlfriend, laughing and feeling—for the first time in like, forever—like they didn't have a care in the world. I just let everything go.

On that late summer evening, the restaurants and the bars had set up tables on the sidewalks, so we had some fun looking at the people there and guessing who were on first dates, who were on "make up" dates, who were seeing someone behind someone else's back. We were laughing, making up stories about the people we were seeing. Just being happy.

We'd stopped in one bar for a quick drink. Neither of us wanted to stay. It was too delightful an evening, made more delightful by the slight alcohol buzz that the drink had given us.

"Why can't every day be like today?" I wanted to know.

Kim smiled. "Just accept it and enjoy it for what it is." She said it lightly, but it was powerful wisdom.

Another block, and the long day piled on top of other long, long days, caught up with me. I was suddenly so beat I didn't feel like I could walk another step. "I think I'm going to call it a night," I told her.

The sun had set, but it was still warm. The streetlights created a comfortable intimacy to the bars and restaurants. Even though I was exhausted, there was a feeling like anything could happen.

"You sure?" Kim asked. "The night is still young."

I laughed. "That, my dear, is a tired pick-up line if I've ever heard one."

She just laughed as we continued walking. We were walking past a restaurant, making our way back toward our car, when we heard a man's voice call out to us. Kim was about to give the man a gentle brush-off when we turned and saw him standing at a bar table with a friend of his. They were both handsome and, quite frankly, the most intriguing men we'd set eyes on probably all year. One of them was wearing the nicest shirt I'd ever seen on a man. It was a crisp lilac pinstripe.

Kim didn't give the brush-off. She turned and glanced at me and arched her eyebrows as if to say, "Well?"

I shrugged. I was tired, and I dipped my head as I looked at her with the slightest of argument…but I was more than willing to get a second wind. Besides, for the lilac shirt alone, I wanted to meet this fellow.

Over a drink, we learned that the gentlemen were local businessmen. Entrepreneurs. Even though stopping to have a drink with them had been completely social, the more we talked with them, the more Kim and I focused on what they did.

We had barely gotten our drinks before we were talking business. The two men, Jason and Patrick, talked about some of the investments they had made, both "brick and mortar" type things as well as tech and software ideas. They wore their success well, obviously comfortable in their own skins.

Kim kept nudging me, prompting me to talk up SaraBear. For some reason though, I felt embarrassed to. Even when Jason asked, "What do you do?," I mumbled something about having my own business, but really I was a nurse. As the music blared and I couldn't hear the conversations around me, Kim, always my greatest supporter, stepped up and told them about SaraBear. She told them what a great product it was, and how it had done so well with Target and other stores before the economy tanked, and how Babies "R" Us was currently on board.

"My sister had a baby not long ago," Patrick said. "She's often complaining about the mess around her house, baby stuff all over. I could've used one when my kids were little."

"Sounds like a smart idea," Jason said.

Even more than SaraBear itself, they became gradually interested in the SaraBear story.

Jason kept smiling and shaking his head. "And you're a nurse?" he asked.

I shrugged. I didn't know whether to be embarrassed or proud the way he asked me. I knew I was always floundering with the business, but he seemed to be genuinely impressed at what I'd managed to do.

"Yeah, well, I'm barely keeping my head above water right now," I said. "So you won't see me straining my arm patting myself on the back."

"I wouldn't be so hard on yourself," Jason said, raising his glass toward me. "Most people don't come close to what you've accomplished—and they lose everything in the process." He shook his head. "You put together a complete production pipeline. Dealt with China. Designed the product. That's incredible."

I glanced down as the three people at the table essentially toasted me. It felt good to have all that effort acknowledged and appreciated. But, the truth of the matter was that no matter how impressive it was, I was still about to go under and lose everything.

So how impressive could it really be?

Jason could see that I wasn't nearly as impressed by my accomplishments as he thought I should be. "I mean it," he said. "Look at what you've done, what you've learned. My God, you dragged yourself up without any idea what you were doing and—"

"And I failed."

He shook his head. "No! You didn't fail. OK, maybe SaraBear hasn't been the success that you dreamed, but you did not fail."

If I could have scripted the exact right people to meet at that moment in my life, I couldn't have done a better job than to have come up with these two guys.

When we got up to leave, we promised to stay in touch. And we did.

"Aren't you glad you didn't decide to just go home when you felt tired before?" Kim asked as we walked away from the bar two hours later.

I smiled from ear to ear, and not because of the alcohol. "I feel like I can just float home," I told her.

She laughed.

"Of course," I added as my smile faded, "that doesn't change anything about all the debt."

"True," Kim said, "but at least you have allies now. I think they might be really helpful to you."

"You think?"

"Absolutely. They know a lot about what you're trying to do."

Sometimes, you don't see that bus coming.

When I woke up at two o'clock that morning, I actually felt a hint of hopefulness aside from the usual terror. Maybe, just maybe, things would work out. Maybe, just maybe, I wasn't the fuck-up I'd come to believe I was.

In October, Ben and I went to meet with the divorce attorney. Even though I didn't *have* to, not legally, as part of my divorce agreement from Benny, I had agreed to accept the burden of all of the debt. I was the one who had gotten us into the mess we'd gotten into. I was determined to be the one to get us out. At least, that was the way I saw it. If I had had one of those really sharp, West Coast divorce lawyers, she would have talked me out of it.

No. I wouldn't have let her.

"You're crazy," she'd have told me. "Do you understand what you're taking on?"

I would have nodded. I was taking on the second and third secured mortgages. All of it. Every penny.

My lawyer—if I would have had that fancy West Coast lawyer, the ones who do the palimony suits for the big stars—would have said, "Don't sign!" But I didn't get into this mess by being sensible. I tried to *act* sensibly once I was in it. I tried to do all the things I needed to do to make it work. But the *decision to get into it* was so far from sensible as you can be. It was all desperate passion. That was what kept me going forward: Passion. Hope. Stupid, stupid things, but the only things worth doing anything for.

I was going forward, because behind me there was only meatloaf.

They could lock me up. They could throw me in a loony bin. They could declare me an enemy of the state. But I was not going back.

"You don't really think the business will sell, do you?" my imaginary lawyer would have asked. And I would have looked her dead in the eye and said, "You bet your ass I do!"

In the deepest part of my heart, I was a true believer. I never, ever, ever stopped believing that the diaper caddy was a great product. I put myself down for being a bad businessperson, a bad planner, or money manager, or whatever else. But the caddy…that was golden. I knew, in the right hands, it would be successful (and I wasn't so crazy to think that my hands were actually the right ones in this case—far from it). I knew I could be like the rare, fortunate few and sell my business. Since the day I invented the SaraBear diaper caddy, I always believed deep down that it was one of the most useful baby products on the market. That belief never went away. That belief, most days, was the only thing that kept me going. But I just *knew* it.

If my "lawyer" had cross-examined me, she'd have asked me why I believed that. "What evidence do you have that it *might* be true?"

Once again, I would look her dead in the eye and say, "Look, if Arnold Schwarzenegger can become governor of California, if a super model can fall in love with Howard Stern, then I can sell this goddamned, pain-in-the-ass, remarkable-it-survived-2009 business!"

Ah, the irrationality of the entrepreneur. It is the reason that smart people take the LSAT and go to law school, or the GRE and go to business school, or the MCAT and go to medical school. Now, those were *smart* things to do if you wanted to make your way in the world. Earn some prestige. Make some good money. Buy an island. Save the world. Whatever.

But it is for the entrepreneurs, the evil geniuses of the world, to hole away in their workrooms, or garages, or basements, and build a better mousetrap, to invent the one thing that they *know beyond a shadow of any reasonable doubt* will earn them fame, fortune, and a way forward from whatever world they live in.

I was like Dr. Frankenstein, crazed in his laboratory as the lightning struck and Igor half-walked, half-crawled to throw the switch. I knew my monster could come to life. But reality was telling me otherwise.

Even now, with that dark chapter of my life far behind me, I have no idea how I made it work; no idea how I managed even day to day, let alone week to week or month to month. I guess the answer is really as simple as can be. I made it work because I had no choice.

It was that or…

I felt like Igor, limping along. My psychological "hump" was affecting me physically. Day after day, I just felt more and more weighted down. I kept trying: I wrote letters. Sent emails. Kept calling. Every company in the juvenile industry with a working phone number, I called 'em.

And then one day…

In early December, I decided to finally reach out to the CEO of a large baby and toy company in California. They had a product that competed with mine for shelf space. And I'd been holding this card in my back pocket, too afraid to play it, that it would come up the Joker. I suspected they'd been watching SaraBear's moves. And so, on a late Friday afternoon, after proofreading my prose a hundred times and whispering a prayer under my breath—I hit the send button and released my email into the hands of the email gods.

To my astonishment and utter surprise, a few hours later, that very same evening, my eyes alighted upon his name in my inbox. He emailed back! But wait, I couldn't read it. What if it said, "Your product is cute, but no thanks." Another tire-kicker. My heart racing a thousand miles a minute, and with no choice left but to look, I double-clicked, and there were the words in black-and-white.

"Melissa. Thanks for writing. I'd like to talk to you more about your product line. Is it in Target only? What is your distribution pipeline?"

Oh. My. God. He was interested!

The way I screamed when I got that email, you would have thought I'd won the lottery! Jesus! He was interested. I got in my car and raced to Kim's house.

We were probably lucky he'd only expressed interest. If the email would have said anything more, we might have exploded on the spot.

All I could think of—once I came down from the shock and high of the email—was "Do not fuck this up, Melissa! Do not!" I looked at Kim. She looked at me.

"How should I play this?"

We were both silent for a moment. Then, at the same instant, we both said, "Jason."

I dialed Jason's number and, when he came on, I steeled my voice. "Hey, Jason," I said. "I need your help."

I hired him on the spot to consult me through the negotiation. I needed a rational spokesperson, an unemotional ally. Someone with the smarts to assemble the pieces of the deal and make certain that every move was made with intelligence. Millions of dollars had passed in front of my eyes as diaper caddies were made, sold, and shipped throughout the world. But the shaky foundation that it took to make those few million would crumble without a sale.

Like any negotiation, there were some snafus and, frighteningly, a couple of times when it seemed like the whole thing might fall through. But Jason stayed calm and steady the whole time, talking me down from the ledge.

"You're doing good," he kept telling me.

He knew exactly what I needed to hear.

I watched and listened and worked with him as he broke my business down into its component parts, dissecting its strengths and weaknesses and what it was really worth in the landscape post-2008. The numbers could work. They could really work. Right there, in black marker on the whiteboard in front of me, was, for the first time in years, a real solution and answer that could actually pay off the debt burden and free me from the weight of the world.

The negotiation, in "deal" timelines, went extremely fast. The lawyers worked swiftly. I raced to get things in order. Jason navigated the terms and guided my negotiation.

Then finally, after weeks, months, and years of stress and worry, after all the fear, all the certainty that life would *never* be without the horrible burden of debt, in the blink of an eye, it was over. The gorilla had left the room.

Four weeks. It was done.

February 4, 2011. I was sitting at a grand wooden conference table in the attorney's office. The attorney's assistant walked in with the paperwork and set it out in front of us.

"Right here, here, again here, and then here," she said, pointing her perfectly manicured finger to lines in need of my signature. One more step, and the deal would be sealed.

"Here?" I asked, trying to hide the unimaginable excitement in my voice, like I'd closed deals a thousand times before. But inside, I could barely contain the joy.

I took a deep breath. "Steady," I told myself. At that moment, I wondered how presidents kept their hands from shaking when they were signing important documents and laws. "Steady."

I signed. Right there. And there. And again there. I signed for those blissful, surreal few minutes, trying to soak in the reality of the fact that I had done it. What 99 percent of myself believed was impossible had come true. "Excellent," my business attorney said, quickly picking up the contract as he chatted with Jason.

I stood up and firmly shook his hand. "That's it?"

He nodded. "That's it."

SaraBear was sold.

"Funds will be wired within twenty-four hours, Melissa. Congratulations."

Chapter 19

BANKRUPTCY CAN KISS MY ASS

Benny was looking at me. He appeared a bit perplexed about the smile on my face. Soda for me, a beer for him, and a pizza between us. The kids had gone over to the pinball machine. The noise of a happily crowded restaurant surrounded us.

We sat in silence a few awkward moments before I couldn't take it anymore. I leaned across the table and looked him warmly in the eyes. "It's over," I said.

He looked at me, confused.

A bit curt, he said, "What do you mean, Melissa, that it's over?"

I lifted up a piece of paper I'd had sitting on my lap. As I slid the paper that read "PAID IN FULL" across the table, I leaned in a little, whispering gloriously, "SaraBear is sold. The secured debt on the house has been paid. All of it." I felt myself physically relax. I exhaled and leaned back. "You're free and clear."

His eyes filled up for a second. I think I saw his lip quiver. "What? Really?"

I nodded. "God's honest truth."

"Whoa, Melissa." He examined the piece of paper from the bank, his eyes widening. He then raised his beer in a toast.

"Well. Congratulations, Melissa."

"Congratulations to you too, Benny."

My family was saved. My children's future was preserved. No matter what we shared for a meal that evening…pizza, filet mignon, or even meatloaf…any meal I ate with my children and their father would have tasted glorious.

CONCLUSION

It took a while for me to "settle in" to a life not filled with stress, fielding the barrage of SaraBear emails while going about my "normal" day. There was a part of me that wondered if, once the relief became familiar, I would miss all of it.

About a month later, the answer came when I woke up one morning after a deep, full night's sleep, without nightmares of tornadoes, without tears at two in the morning, without my stomach churning and anxiety pounding in my chest, without fear and worry. With my kids sleeping peacefully in their rooms adjacent to mine. With all the debt paid off. With no more collection-calls from the credit card companies, with a nice hard-earned balance in my savings account and a pile of "Paid in Full" papers on my desk that I had to look at every day to remind myself of the ending that actually came true…

The answer was clear.

No. I most definitely would not miss it.

And I finally began to sleep.

***

My mother being diagnosed with terminal cancer at fifty-nine, when I was just pregnant with Sara, changed the paradigm of my life. She lived way longer than we had any reason to hope she would. Still, her dying four years later, at sixty-two, changed everything.

I saw her live only part of a life. She was not only robbed of length of time she lived, but in the kind of life she'd lived. I'm not convinced she ever really expressed who she truly was, ever got to embrace life in all its messy, wonderful glory. But for her, life was content, safe. This worked for her. Given the childhood she endured, it was truly a miracle she was blessed with the life she and my father made together.

I see now, though, that her illness and eventual death was a catalyst for my revolt from my handed-down, conventional, by-the-rules existence. The cruel tragedy of her dying before getting to see the lives of her grandchildren blossom convinced me that no dream within reach should ever be deferred. The future is just that—the future. It is not a guarantee.

There are no guarantees.

I wanted more from my life than what my mom had. I couldn't put that into words right then. I was whipsawed between grief and my own desire of starting a family, the loss of what was and the bittersweet happiness of what was to be. Despite the sadness, I was madly in love with my children and wanted nothing more than to be a really good wife and mother. I had the best role model imaginable in my own mom.

But somewhere inside, the real Melissa made an oath to herself. She invited herself to the party. She swore that she would *not* live only part of a life. That she would somehow break the pattern for her own daughter. And the seeds of this woman were planted in the form of invention. A simple, practical, no-one-else-had-thought-of-it-before diaper caddy named after a beautiful little girl named Sara.

ACKNOWLEDGMENTS

To acknowledge is to say thank you. First, I thank my beautiful children. Sara and Nathaniel—to be your mother is a privilege, and to love you and watch you grow is the greatest gift ever bestowed to me. Being a parent, having children, forces us to strive to be a better person. We become accountable to a higher standard. Even at our lowest lows, we have to keep our chin up and exemplify what we would want for our children. Having children completes a life. Without you, I just wouldn't have cared nearly as much, and the one-in-a-million success would have never come true. Thank you, kittens.

(P.S.: You can read this book when you turn, say, thirty. Sorry, I drop the ef-bomb far too much.)

To Dave, my dear friend—you also lost your mother too soon. And you understand the angst, the organic invitation to dig down deep and find and meet who we *really* are, the importance of feeling the raw nerve endings of life and exploring all life has to offer. Thank you. For supporting me, telling me like it is, and always calling a spade a spade. You're totes awesome!

To my beautiful sister, Amy. Your heart is made of gold just like Moms. Thank you for always supporting me, even when I'm kind of a bitch.

Kim. My Kimmy…an example of a true friend. No judging, always encouraging, honest. Thank you for believing in me, never fazed by my pitty-parties. Thank you for everything.

To Jason and PT. Thank you for enticing us into your world that evening. I love you both.

To D and A, my barometers in life on very different levels. Thank you for seeing through my bullshit and to who I really am and bringing out the absolute best and pathetic worst in me: both necessary in any person's journey to a fully lived life.

Thank you to Jill for your praise, editing and cleaning up my-annoying-and-criminal-use-of-commas-and-dashes, not to mention my repeated violations between past and present tense.

Ann and Hans, thank you for believing in the SaraBear Diaper Caddy® and its potential. Without you it may have ended before seeing its success. I will always appreciate your rescue.

Catherine, thanks for proudly standing along side me as I looked like the kid at a homemade lemonade stand. And to Uncle Matt, who, if I remember correctly, originally coined baby Sara as *SaraBear*.

To Nancy Kimball, thank you, also, for believing in me even though you may not have really believed I knew what I was doing. (I didn't, almost the whole time.)

To anyone I forgot to acknowledge, I apologize. But it's probably a miracle I remembered everything that I did.

And finally, there would have been no happy ending were it not for you. With the deepest appreciation a person can feel, Stanley, I thank you.

ABOUT THE AUTHOR

Melissa Coleman Bramlage is an entrepreneur, retired registered nurse, mother and lawn-mower extraordinaire. Founder and former CEO of SaraBear®, her patented diaper caddy line and popular brand was acquired in 2011. Melissa knew her experience in creating and marketing SaraBear could be eye-opening and inspirational for other would-be entrepreneurs. But for a long while the wounds were still too fresh, the exhilarating highs too high, the dark lows too low.

By 2013, she was finally ready. It was time to tell her story. So, tell it she does, with candor and heart, revealing a journey of personal transformation by way of a one-in-a-million triumph.

Melissa knows in the marrow of her bones and the pit of her stomach that to be a successful entrepreneur you have to be up before the sun, ready to face the day with all its potential joy and heartache. You have to shrug off the conventional advice of friends and family. You have to confront the road "less traveled" with the faith that your resume will read like hers, "Doer of many things, none of which seem to have any relation to one another – unless you possess the eyes to truly see!"

These days, when she's not obsessively in quest of the perfect green lawn, Melissa can often be spotted along the country roads of upstate New York, with a drooling mastiff hanging its head out the window, as she proudly drives her embarrassed kids to and from the ball fields of their glorious youth.

www.ingramcontent.com/pod-product-compliance
Lightning Source LLC
Chambersburg PA
CBHW071501040426
42444CB00008B/1440